TRAVOLTA
TO
KEATON

By Rex Reed

TRAVOLTA TO KEATON

VALENTINES & VITRIOL

PEOPLE ARE CRAZY HERE

BIG SCREEN, LITTLE SCREEN

CONVERSATIONS IN THE RAW

DO YOU SLEEP IN THE NUDE?

TRAVOLTA TO KEATON

by

REX REED

WILLIAM MORROW AND COMPANY, INC.
NEW YORK 1979

Grateful thanks to Paramount Pictures Corp., Universal City Studios, Inc., and Columbia Pictures Industries for photographs.

Library of Congress Cataloging in Publication Data

Reed, Rex.
Travolta to Keaton.

1. Moving-picture actors and actresses—United States—Biography—Addresses, essays, lectures.
2. Moving-pictures—United States—Biography—Addresses, essays, lectures. I. Title.
PN1998.A2R35 1979 791.43'028'0922 [B] 78-27028
ISBN 0-688-03434-9

BOOK DESIGN CARL WEISS

Printed in the United States of America.

First Edition

1 2 3 4 5 6 7 8 9 10

CONTENTS

TRAVOLTA TO KEATON

1

JOHN TRAVOLTA

JOHN TRAVOLTA STRETCHES HIS COLT LEGS ON TOP OF A GLASS coffee table to work out the kinks, tugs at his turtleneck sweater, fingers the Kirk Douglas dimple in his Cinemascope chin, and ponders the latest ordeal in what upwardly mobile movie stars have come to expect from life in a fishbowl. At twenty-three, he's the hottest thing to hit Teenybopper Heaven since space shoes, corn dogs and peanut butter. Move over, Elvis. There's a new pelvis in town. He's Vinnie Barbarino, a blue-collar punk from Brooklyn on TV's "Welcome Back, Kotter," and Tony Manero, a blue-collar disco dancer from Brooklyn in *Saturday Night Fever*. But somewhere beneath that duck grease, there's a John Travolta struggling to get out. He won't be nominated for any Pulitzers in scientific analysis, but he just might be nominated for an Oscar. Unlike Vinnie and Tony, he makes complete sentences, uses the right verbs, even knows words like "motivate" and "redundant." He's no dese-dems-and-dose cretin. And —shock of shocks to the throngs of screaming teen-agers who mob him—he's not too tripped out on new fame to keep playing Vinnie and Tony off-screen, either.

"I can sense what the public wants just from the way I've been treated by the press," he says softly. "They start out with 'Now don't you think . . .' and I get hostile. What they're really saying is 'This is what I think.' They don't really care what I think. They come in with the attitude 'C'mon, baby, make a mistake, tell us something dumb like the roles you play.' They forget about the work that went into creating those roles. On 'Kotter' the schedule is very light. I could almost do it in my sleep. I work about three or four hours a day, then do a dress rehearsal on Monday and tape the show on Tuesday. With the movie, I worked like hell. For twelve weeks, I was up at five every morning and didn't get home until ten at night, then on weekends I was rehearsing the dance numbers. I needed stamina I didn't have. I certainly didn't get it from the 'Kotter' schedule. It was grueling. I went into training for five months, dancing three hours a day and running two miles a day. I had to lose twenty pounds to get what you see on the screen. I hired the boxer who trained Sylvester Stallone for *Rocky*. When I started, I couldn't even do one of the knee bends I do in the film. By the end of five months, I had a whole new body. I don't have a high energy level, but when I read the script, I said, 'If he's supposed to be the best disco dancer, I want to be the best disco dancer.' I knew how to dance, but I wasn't that good. I really had to work to push my energy level. Also, I knew a lot was riding on me. This movie is probably the most important step in my career."

Oblivious to the work involved in creating the illusion of a finger-popping, hip-grinding dance machine, the public bought the act and made Travolta an instant pop sensation. It is not, he points out quickly, an overnight success. The baby in a family of thespians from Englewood, New Jersey, he was sent by his mother, a local actress and director, to Gene Kelly's brother Fred for tap-dancing lessons when he was five years old. When he was six, his sister got a part in the road company of *Gypsy* with Ethel Merman and he followed her on tour, hanging around backstage until the wee hours of the morning, hooked on show business. At twelve, he made his stage debut in a serious Actors Studio production of Frank Gilroy's *Who'll Save the Plowboy?* At sixteen, he played Hugo in *Bye Bye, Birdie*. That was 1970. A tour of *Grease* and a nine-month stint in the Broadway musical *Over Here!* with the Andrews Sisters followed. "I had no idea any of this would happen," he says, looking back on those days of anonymity and sweat. "My manager said, 'Let's try Hollywood and see what happens.' I had been offered six hundred dollars a week to do *The Ritz* on Broadway and that was the most money I had ever heard of. I told him, 'I've never turned down anything this big, man,' but I went to California and took the gamble, and four months later I got the 'Kotter' show. I've been incredibly lucky."

After three seasons on the show, it's obvious that Travolta is tired of running a comb through his D.A. haircut and saying great lines like "Geez." TV makes you an instant celebrity, but it eats your time like a crocodile. "I've given them three good years, but I wouldn't play a character on Broadway that long. I've got nothing left to prove on that show. It's glorious what's happened and I'm proud of what I created with Vinnie Barbarino, but I want to do other things that turn me on." He could have made a fortune, but chose instead to act in a summer package of *Bus Stop* during his vacation from "Kotter." Then along came the one-million-dollar package deal from the Stigwood Organization to do three feature films. *Saturday Night Fever* and the forthcoming *Grease,* filmed during vacation breaks from the "Kotter" show, are the first two. Next, he'll do a complete change of pace in a "sensitive love story with Lily Tomlin." Lily says she'll kill him if he reveals the plot.

OK. It looks good on paper. But that's not a lot of money for the kind of star attraction Travolta has become. And, he adds, he's still not as rich as Elton John. "By the time I get my paycheck, there's not much left. If you take the gross figures, you'd think I was rolling in money. But the breakdown would astound you. I pay 50 percent of my income to managers, business managers, lawyers, agents, secretaries and staff. On the remaining 50 percent, I'm in the 50-percent tax bracket. That leaves me with nothing. Last year, I was living in a one-bedroom apartment. For the amount of money that was coming in, I was no better off than I was seven years ago in New York. So I sat down and had a long talk with myself. I said, 'Hell, John, you're allowed to change with your success. Your fans want you to change. If not, what are you working so hard for?' So instead of a house, I bought an airplane."

A what? "Yeah." He grins. "While I was in *Over Here!* on Broadway, I took flying lessons at Teterboro Airport. I have a license to pilot a single-engine plane. I own one of those, but now I also own a commercial DC-3. I also own a classic Thunderbird. Now I go to get the plane fixed and they charge me four times the amount that was on my estimate. I know it's because of my name. I took the T-Bird and they kept it for nine months. When they see me coming, the price of parts goes up. They're not even subtle about it. They just rip me off overtly. Success turned the things I really love into nightmares. I had a potential lawsuit on my plane, I couldn't get my T-Bird out of the shop. I truly felt frustrated before *Saturday Night Fever* came out. The average person will probably read this and think, Oh, I wish I had such problems, right? But when you're in whatever reality you're in, those are the problems."

Seven years ago, he was living with a group of struggling actors in a condemned building with erratic heat and a broken elevator. "I was seventeen, I had just quit school, and New York was a gigantic playground. But now I like California better. No matter where you live out there, there's sunshine outside and a palm tree under your window." When he first arrived in Los Angeles, he was so scared he carried a bottle of Maalox around in his pocket. Now he's so hot they mob him in the street and try to rip his clothes off, but he's ditched the stomach emulsions. "I had to learn to protect myself. The first thing I did when I got to New York to promote *Saturday Night Fever* was walk down Fifth Avenue. Every fifth person would recognize me and yell, 'Hey, there's John Travolta!' It was great. I got off on it. When it's least appealing is when you're eating and somebody comes up in a restaurant and takes your fork out of your hand. I used to think, Well, all this noise is temporary and they'll get tired of me and go on to somebody else. But it hasn't happened. So now I know it isn't going to end unless I change my face. I might as well live with it. I feel good enough about myself to go out and have a good time and ignore the mobs. My phone calls are screened. I never register my name or room number in a hotel I'm staying in. I have an unlisted phone and I've hired a company to handle my fan mail. I don't have enough money to answer ten thousand letters a week myself. Think what the stamps would cost. If I go to a movie, I call up ahead and the manager sneaks me in ahead of the crowd. I still get the nuts. I've got one eighteen-year-old who hangs around my apartment building in L.A. She broke into my building recently and knocked on my door at six in the morning and it was a day I didn't have to get up at six, too. I had to call the police. Here's the way I look at it. If it all ends for me tomorrow, they'll still remember my face. So I've decided not to stop my life or hide from the public. I'm handling it pretty well."

Nine months of analysis helped him cope. Then there was the calming influence of a love affair with the late Diana Hyland, an excellent actress he met and fell in love with when she played his mother in a TV movie called "The Boy in the Plastic Bubble." "Diana was seventeen years older than I was, but we never knew the difference. We talked all day and all night about everything. I have never been so fulfilled in my life and when she died I felt like I lost my center. I haven't found anyone like her since. When I made *Grease,* they wrote that I was romantically linked with Olivia Newton-John, which was totally ridiculous. When I make the movie with Lily, they'll probably write that I'm having a love affair with her. I took Carly Simon to the *Saturday Night Fever* premiere. Now the next rumor will be that she's leaving James Taylor for me. The truth is, I haven't been able to meet anyone since Diana. Younger women no longer interest me."

That will come as a disappointment to Travolta's teen-age worshipers, but not as much of a letdown as his firm belief that "in the overall scheme of things, the teenybopper following means nothing. You have to please yourself in this life. For a long time, I played all the games and acted out whatever people wanted from me because I was ambitious. Now I want to do more adult roles. If that means taking a chance on losing some of my followers, it's a gamble I'm willing to face. All I can do is the best work I know how to do as a serious actor. I'll never satisfy everyone, but if I try only to satisfy the audience who want me to go through life as Vinnie Barbarino, I'll end up in the toilet. I never denied the characters I played the way Henry Winkler kept denying The Fonz in print and that's made it easier for me to play other parts. You can't tell people what you want to be, you have to show them. The way I look at it, if I can please an adult audience, then the kids will grow up, too."

The adults who are cheering their way through *Saturday Night Fever* no longer call him John Revolta. Some of the female hysterics who mail him requests to autograph their panties are old enough for Medicare. What the hell. Yesterday, the bubble-gum brigade. Tomorrow, the world.

2

FRED ZINNEMANN

JANE FONDA AND VANESSA REDGRAVE TAKE THEIR BOWS, LILLIAN Hellman and young producer Richard Roth get photographed at parties in their honor, and the real star of *Julia* stands alone with his hands in his pockets, high above the city he's just conquered, away from the spotlight. He is Fred Zinnemann, one of the great, great film directors, and at the age of seventy, he wears the serene, bemused look of a veteran who's been on the front lines before.

For a man who has just made the fall season's first full-scale smash-hit movie, Zinnemann looks more like an aging jockey or somebody's kindly grandfather than a director of the first magnitude. But underneath that calm, soft-spoken frame the size of a kitchen stool, a giant is waiting to get out. He works slowly, meticulously and rarely, which partially explains why he turns out only one picture every five or six years. But when he does work, the result is *High Noon*, or *The Member of the Wedding*, or *From Here To Eternity*, or *A Man For All Seasons*, or *The Nun's Story*, to name just a few of his classics. "My problem," he says, the morning after *Julia* has taken New York by storm, "is finding good stories. Once I find something that moves me sufficiently to want to communicate it to others, then I sometimes take years getting it on the screen in the right way. I'm not interested in personal glory. I'm only interested in making good movies and at my age, I'm not sure how many I've got left in me."

Perfecting *Julia* wasn't easy, even for a man with Zinnemann's esteem. There were rumors that he feuded with both Lillian Hellman, on whose memoir *Pentimento* the film was based, and producer Richard Roth. Zinnemann is the portrait of diplomacy, yet he doesn't flinch from the question. "You know, I don't do many interviews. I don't open up easily and it's difficult to get through all of my defenses. The press usually bends your quotes and uses you badly. But since I agreed to do this one, I will try to be honest. The truth is, I was not the first choice to direct *Julia*. Richard Roth initiated the project, bought the option to the movie rights, got Alvin Sargent to write it, talked Fox into putting up the money, talked Jane Fonda into playing Lillian. Up to that point, he was totally in charge. Sydney Pollack was the original director, but he got tied up with *Bobby Deerfield* and they paid him off. That's when I entered the picture. Sargent, Roth and I went to Martha's Vineyard and spent three days with Lillian Hellman to perfect the final draft. She made changes, voiced her objections and hangups, and we tried very hard to satisfy her. Then, when we started shooting, I invited her to London as a guest three times. She said she was not well enough, but I noticed she was well enough to travel to Egypt and to the Academy Awards. So much for that. Now she says I never invited her, but I have cables to prove it. Then when the film was completed, she sent word that she'd like it sent to Martha's Vineyard so she could see it. Which is absurd. I was not going to ship a brand-new film off to Martha's Vineyard since I had no idea what conditions it would be shown under. How far do you have to go to kowtow to Lillian Hellman? When I worked on Andre Malraux's *Man's Fate*, I had to remove one character completely. Malraux said, 'A movie is not a book, what works for literature does not always work on the screen—it's your movie, do what you must do!' If Malraux had enough confidence, you'd think Miss Hellman would, too. I think she behaved very badly. After the film's success, she didn't bother to even write or phone me to say thank you.

"As for the producer," he continues, "I think Richard Roth is perceptive, intelligent and has very good taste. But he wants to be an instant David Selznick. Gradually, a friction developed. At one point, I offered to resign, but Fox wouldn't accept my resignation. I was forced to allow the producer to see the daily rushes, but our artistic contact was curtailed when he was banned from the set at my request. Except for a few like Selznick and Sam Goldwyn, not many producers know anything about making movies. When they start asking you what you're shooting and why, it's time to take a stand. I don't mean for this to sound like a harangue against Richard Roth. I like him in many ways, but he turned out not to know a great deal about the physical production problems on a European location. A producer should be the man who makes it easy for the director to get on with it. Once you're out there commanding vast numbers of people and directing the placement of tons of expensive equipment, you are on your own as a director and whatever happens, I must in the final analysis be responsible for my films, good or bad."

Nothing soothes wounds like success, so it's safe to say that the conflicts have been resolved. *Julia* has everyone speaking again, and Zinnemann's reputation as a monolith among directors is safely secured. He's one of the few directors who gets contractual control over sets, costumes, casting, all details. He's had to fight for this autonomy. In his Hollywood salad days, he had "a very rough time with Stanley Kramer. He's the kind of man who invariably says he saves other people's films in the cutting room. He still claims credit for *High Noon* and *Member of the Wedding*. The truth is, he went around telling everyone *High Noon* was lousy until it became a great smash hit. Then he took credit for its success, of course. He wasn't even around during *Wedding,* and when I did *The Men* with Brando, he overdramatized and sentimentalized it by adding Dimitri Tiomkin music and making violent cuts. In those days, I had no control over anything, so I just say I directed those movies. I never say I made them. The problem with producers is that they buy up properties to promote themselves into that position of producer, but they get on the set and all they do is get in the way."

Up to *High Noon*, Zinnemann says he was known as an "art-house director—which meant the pictures were pretty good, but nobody went to see them. My own strength began after *High Noon*. I've been fighting the system ever since. In Hollywood, if you make one successful picture, they call it an accident. If you make two successful pictures in a row, they call it a miracle. It gets more grotesque each time around. When I did *The Sundowners*, they wanted me to make it in Arizona. It was set in Australia. They said, 'We'll bring in the kangaroos.' I had to persuade them I was making a picture about people, not landscapes. On *The Nun's Story*, they said, 'Who wants to see a documentary about how to be a nun?' Then Audrey Hepburn said she wanted to do it, and I had no further problems. I don't know what my reputation is in Hollywood now. My agent says I can get a job anytime I want one, but none of the good stories about America have worked out, so that's why I haven't worked in America in so long."

He abandoned *Hawaii* after two years because he "never got a decent script," a fact the subsequent film directed by George Roy Hill proved. *Custer* was from the Indian point of view, a premise considered unpopular by Darryl F. Zanuck, who wanted to show Custer as a traditionally whitewashed hero. The project was abandoned after the budget zoomed to $18 million. So Zinnemann has concentrated his work in Europe. Shortly after he won an Oscar for *A Man for All Seasons*, he "began to feel people no longer cared about my films. I was out in the cold. My kind of films were considered too old-fashioned. Then I spent three years on *Man's Fate*. I rehearsed with the actors, the sets were built and dressed, over four million dollars had already been spent on it, and MGM canceled the film to cut costs. I was foolish enough to make the deal with no signed contracts. It taught me a handshake means nothing. It ended up in a nasty lawsuit and it was a shattering experience that took up four and a half years of my life."

About the only people Zinnemann has not had problems with in his career are actors. They praise him to the skies. "The way I work with actors is to make them feel I respect their talents and instincts and then I ask them to tell me their concept of the characters they are playing, rather than impose my concept on them. The result is that actors are thus freed from inhibitions and they make astounding contributions." He's gotten along with some difficult temperaments. Ethel Waters "was not an easy person to argue with. She had learned all of her blocking for *Member of the Wedding* from the stage, so when she would move three steps away on a line she would end up out of camera range. Each time I tried to help her, she'd roll her eyes to the heavens and say, 'God is my director!' How can you argue with that? She was a very sad person. Between scenes, she sat all alone in her dressing room, listening to her old phonograph records." Each actor, he says, has a different need. "With Audrey Hepburn, I had to loosen her up. She was too nice, too pretty, too much like a fashion model to play a disillusioned nun." Gary Cooper? "You looked at him on the screen like you'd watch a child or a kitten. He had magic. The only time he was in trouble was when he tried to act." Montgomery Clift? "He was difficult, but he was so exciting it didn't matter. He had a thin skin, he needed protection, sometimes he was totally helpless."

And now, Vanessa Redgrave and Jane Fonda, in *Julia*? "With Vanessa, you don't talk at all. She is absolutely fantastic. The scene where she tells Jane she has a baby—in the middle, she starts chomping on a mouthful of caviar. That was totally her idea, and it is one of the magic moments in *Julia*. I told her at the very beginning, 'I'd love to do this with you, but you must promise never to bring your politics to the set.' There was enough bad feeling about her already. She tried to sell that newspaper of hers once, but everybody laughed and she finally gave it up. With Jane, we also had it out early. I told her this would not be a political soapbox movie. Jane was disappointed, but the more you give in to her, the more domineering she becomes. If Lillian Hellman had been along with Vanessa and Jane, I don't think I could have handled it."

Zinnemann has a reputation for making strenuous demands on his co-workers. "Many people are nervous with me, because I stretch them, but I ask nothing of them I wouldn't ask of myself." The man who carried Billy Wilder's camera in Berlin, and learned his philosophy from John Ford and Robert Flaherty in his fledgling days in Hollywood, has earned his place in the front ranks of American filmmakers. "Flaherty told me, 'Have a vision of what you want and stick with it. Never get sidetracked by compromises!' And John Ford told me, 'Don't give them too much extra film, then they can't cut it a different way!' " The doctor's son from Vienna has done it his way, and at seventy, most folks think, there's nothing he can't do. "But," he adds, smiling shyly, "on the first day of every film, I still get butterflies."

3

GERALDINE FITZGERALD

STEAMING PORRIDGE. FROSTY MOORS. CRISP IRISH LINEN. PLAIN talk, no nonsense, and nourishing barley soup. These are the images one conjures from Geraldine Fitzgerald. She's too old to be called a colleen, but she's still a handsome, hearty broth of a woman with the same radish-cheeked complexion, sensible carriage and blarney-kissed humor of her native Ireland that made her an instant commodity back in the Forties on the Warner Brothers back lot. She still shows up on the late show in classics like *Dark Victory* and *Wuthering Heights*, but the winter of her years has now evolved into a new career—first as a character actress lighting up New York stages in recent hit revivals of *Ah, Wilderness!* and *Long Day's Journey into Night*, and at this moment as the rage of a new nightclub act that is packing them in at a tiny, smoke-filled cabaret called Brothers and Sisters. From the Brothers Warner to the Brothers and Sisters, she's come full circle.

It's impossible to describe what Geraldine Fitzgerald does to mesmerize an audience. Playwright Arthur Laurents says, "She can't sing a note, but she destroys you!" Go figure that one out. Geraldine says, "I've only got about four tones, but it's not what you've got, it's what you do with it that counts." She does plenty. She takes the ambition every man on the street has to sing, adds a fantastic acting technique and makes what she calls "street songs" personal and moving.

"These are the songs I used to sing as a young girl in the streets of Dublin and in the Irish countryside. I have done a lot of research and I find audiences enjoy learning where these songs came from. 'Greensleeves' was really written by Henry the Eighth. 'Danny Boy' is about the potato famine. 'The White Cliffs of Dover' was a World War Two song sung by mothers in air-raid shelters under the subways to put their children to sleep while the bombs fell on London. I call them street songs because they can be performed anywhere, without microphones or stages or props. It's the most basic kind of popular art."

To aid her, she's got a pianist who plays for Benny Goodman and Gerry Mulligan, and a percussionist who fills in on everything from saxophones and wind instruments to an exotic Irish drum called a *bodhran,* which looks like the pans miners used when panning for gold.

From such bizarre remnants, she has assembled an unusual act that leaves audiences screaming with applause. "It's all been quite an accident, really. It all started when I went to audition for the role of Joanne Woodward's mother in Paul Newman's film *Rachel, Rachel.* I wore a gray wig, and they thought I was the new nanny. Joanne was terrifically pleased to see me and said, 'Thank goodness you're here.' I said, 'Don't you want to know what I've been doing lately?' and she said, 'Oh, no, we don't care about your references, just go right into the children's room.'

"It took her a few minutes before she roared with laughter and said, 'Oh, my God, it's Geraldine!' Well, what happened was they rewrote one of the men's parts and made me a crazy revival-tent preacher, and I had to sing in the scene. There was a vocal teacher named Andy Anselmo on the set that day, and he said he could teach me to organize the sounds so they wouldn't fly all over the place, and I'd be able to express myself musically the way Rex Harrison does! That's really how it all began."

Most people wonder why a mature woman, whose aunt was the woman Sean O'Casey wrote all of his great plays for, with a rich husband (Stuart Scheftel, former publisher of the *New York Post*) and a comfortable life would want to toil for a living in a shoebox-sized nightclub. "Because," she says, wide-eyed with surprise at the insouciance of such a question, "I really, really love to sing. My family hated the idea. At first, Andy took me out to these remote clubs in the slag heaps of New Jersey, and I'd get up and sing 'More,' and they weren't very polite. My family would tag along loyally and say, 'Don't do this to yourself!' But I have always wanted to sing.

"I'm probably the only mother alive whose lullabies were rejected by her own children in their nursery. But serious people in the theater like Julie Harris, Henry Fonda, Eileen Heckart and James Whitmore are all doing one-person shows. That's how this act started.

"I had to devise my own way of working because nobody is writing parts for actresses my age anymore. In this business, if you aren't thirty, you must at least give the impression of being thirty to be considered usable, especially if you're a woman. When a woman reaches that middle period, when she stops looking twenty but isn't old yet, she has a terrible time finding enough work to sustain her creative needs. If I had stayed in films, I'd be all washed up. That's why so many celebrated film actresses end up being so miserable and confused. They are expected to look the same forever. They're never allowed to develop into whatever they become. Audiences still want to see Bette Davis, but when they get into the movie they're disappointed because they aren't seeing the Bette Davis of thirty years ago."

Geraldine Fitzgerald's own Hollywood days were less than glorious. She was poisoned by George Sanders in *Uncle Harry*, terrorized by Peter Lorre and Sydney Greenstreet in *Three Strangers*, swindled by John Garfield in *Nobody Lives Forever* and gave up her life as a spy for Alan Ladd in *O.S.S.* They could never figure out what kind of slot to fit her into. "I wasn't exactly this, I wasn't exactly that, and Jack Warner was never very good at developing what a person really was. Bette Davis was the only one who got to do everything, and she had to fight like hell to do it." Geraldine had beauty, brains, talent and an unusual, chocolate-syrup voice. For a while, she was the "best friend." Then she was an Ingrid Bergman type. She was never herself. "The place where I could have broken through was *The Maltese Falcon* because John Huston would have presented me as a siren, but I was having a row with Jack Warner at the time. If I had played that, then Warners would probably have said, 'Ah, yes, that's what she is, at last we know!'

"What I should have done is what Humphrey Bogart told me to do. He said, 'Do everything they throw at you and maybe you'll click in one of them!' But I was always trying to get back to the theater or worrying about whether what I was doing was art. That's not the way to have a career. I didn't have the vaguest idea how to survive in Hollywood. Bette Davis fought all these violent battles, but she staged her greatest fights at a period when she was big box office. I didn't have any muscle, and I didn't have a big enough body of work for the public to support me. I made awful mistakes, but looking back on it, it was my own ignorance that prevented me from becoming a star."

She had grown up in the intellectual Dublin theater—that Irish equivalent to London's Bloomsbury group. O'Casey. Yeats. Synge. James Joyce. They shook the world. Total integrity. Nothing vulgar like interviews in the press or (God forbid!) money. The young Geraldine's pretty head was full of arty plans. She played with Orson Welles's Mercury Theatre in *Heartbreak House* and *Julius Caesar*. Then Welles decided to combine all five of Shakespeare's Henry kings into one play, and there was no role for her, so she accepted an offer from Hal Wallis to travel to Hollywood for a screen test.

While she was working with Bette Davis and Bogart in *Dark Victory*, the Mercury went bankrupt and she was stranded in Lotus Land in a state of frustration and terror.

"It was 1938 when all sorts of dazzling people were at Warners—Ben Hecht, Aldous Huxley, William Faulkner. Dorothy Parker used to sit in a tiny room while Joan Crawford slashed red lines through her dialogue. I used to think these people were standing up to the system like I was, but they weren't. They were giving in when they had to, which was the right way. The answer to people like me is don't go to Hollywood. Don't have the hubris to think you can make it work with integrity when you are, in fact, dealing with an industry.

"Moviemaking is not too different from manufacturing airplane motors, except it's people, instead of machinery, being turned out on an assembly line. Igor Stravinsky was there working for Walt Disney, and he didn't have anything to do with anybody, but he wasn't in the position of having to find parts or build a career. Now I read in the papers that Miss Somebody is going into TV or the movies, and she's determined to do only good things. I just laugh, because I know these youngsters are going to suffer. By the time I figured it all out, the war was on, I was separated from my first husband with a child to support, and I couldn't stay on suspension any longer. I had to earn a living. So I did everything I was offered, but by that time I had lost the momentum and the contacts, and my career was in a shambles."

So she left Hollywood, married Stuart Scheftel, whom she met in 1943, when he was running for Congress on the Lower East Side, and after a long struggle to keep a career alive, she retired. Her daughter, Susie, was born and she stayed home. "Then when I did start to pursue a career again, I was able to do it as the person I had become. If anyone was looking for the lady in *Wuthering Heights* they didn't find her.

"One day when I was playing Gary Cooper's wife in *Ten North Frederick,* Norma Shearer came to see me. I'll never forget what she told me: 'I admire your courage, Geraldine, starting all over again in character roles. It's something I will never do, because time has passed me by.' That's the saddest thing about Hollywood. It has no memory."

She's not a woman who lives in the past, but when she thumbs through her old scrapbooks, funny memories come back to prick her. "Here's a photo of Orson Welles and me. We had a great flirtation that didn't come to much, but we never had the great love affair we were rumored to have had at the time. The rumor is that Michael Lindsay-Hogg, my son, is really Orson's son. I've never discussed it for publication, but I can understand the rumor because there is a resemblance." Michael is now a successful director himself, having just completed a film of Muriel Spark's *The Abbess of Crewe* with Glenda Jackson, Melina Mercouri, Geraldine Page, Sandy Dennis and Anne Jackson.

"It isn't true, but I can tell you how it got started. During the war, Michael's father, Eddie Lindsay-Hogg, was in New York raising money for the Red Cross, and I was out in Hollywood staying with

Orson. We were just good friends. He was having a terrific love affair with Dolores del Rio, and they kept an apartment in town. One night he came to the house he owned where I was staying to pick up some things, the servants were away, and I was in bed with a terrible case of career depression, in an advanced state of pregnancy. So Orson came in and said, 'Get up, get dressed, and I'll take you out to a smashing supper at Chasen's and tell you about what I'm going to direct for my first movie.'

"So here I am living in Orson's house, and the two of us showed up at Chasen's with me terrifically pregnant, and that's where the rumor started." The movie turned out to be *Citizen Kane,* the structure was an idea he got from his houseguest, and she ended up with a scandal. "So at the bottom of this whole heap of people who gave birth to that classic film was your heavily pregnant old friend Geraldine." And that's how Hollywood autobiographies are born.

4

BURT REYNOLDS

Burt Reynolds saved himself one hundred dollars recently. He sat on the sofa in a dark room at the Waldorf-Astoria in a white cashmere sweater, suede movie-star jeans and cowboy boots and used me as a psychiatrist. We made an odd cast for a two-character psychodrama: a New York critic who never cared much for Burt Reynolds movies and an ex-football jock from Florida State University whose father was a chief of police and who made millions playing raunchy, conceited apes and becoming the idol of the plastic-dinette set. But the meeting was a revelation. We both learned a lot about Burt Reynolds.

He was in New York to promote *The End*, a black comedy about a man dying of a terminal blood disease. It's wild, unpredictable, outrageous, irreverent and not for everybody. But Burt Reynolds loves it, even if his fans may not, and the reason has nothing to do with money.

"It took six years and a tremendous amount of courage to make it. It was originally written for Woody Allen. Then they wanted Dustin Hoffman. Paul Newman had it for a year and got talked out of it. When I said I wanted to do it, they said, 'A guy has to run up to you on the beach at the end and say, "We got the wrong X ray." ' No way is Burt Reynolds gonna die. The last time I died was in *Hustle*. It did ten million dollars in the first ten days and then the word got out that I died in it and it dropped dead, too, at the box office. But I refused to compromise. Of course my audience will still be waiting for the car chase, so I put one in as a kind of Hitchcock gimmick. Sort of an homage to Burt Reynolds." He grins, but he's dead serious.

"College kids love the irreverence. It's easier to laugh at death when you're twenty than it is for me now, since I've passed forty. But one middle-aged woman came up to me and said, 'I have breast cancer and I don't find this film funny at all.' Well, I have no way to defend this film at all. I said, 'Lady, I respect your pain and my heart goes out to you, but I don't know what to say. I will die too someday. We all die.' Howard Hughes couldn't buy his way out of it. Onassis couldn't stop it. But when the time comes, I think I know how I'll react—exactly like the guy in the movie. I will be a coward; I'll immediately try to make a bargain with God. I'll offer him anything which I will immediately renege on. I'd like to die publicly, like Hubert Humphrey. I'd go on the 'Tonight' show and ask everybody in America to send me cards and letters, and then I'd like a Friars Club roast and eleven eulogies about what a great guy I was."

He's not just whistling the funeral march. A few years ago he almost died with a condition that was later diagnosed as hypoglycemia. "I was tired, manic-depressive, hyperventilating, fainting all the time. During that year some hysterical thing happened. One night my heart started pounding so hard I thought my chest was caving in. So I called an ambulance. Now I'm on so many movie-star maps that everybody in Hollywood knows where my house is. Every tourist from Kokomo can find it, but this ambulance couldn't find it. They passed three times, so I dragged myself out on the lawn and waved at them and they went by again. So I lay down in the street until they stopped.

"We got to the hospital and they pumped something into my veins and shoved me into a room with three old Jewish guys playing cards.

I was almost unconscious at this point when suddenly I felt a hand tapping against the intravenous bottle. I looked up and this old guy said, 'You play gin rummy?' I said, 'I'm dying.' To which he replied, 'We're all dying.' So we all ended up in wheelchairs playing cards while the nurse asked me for an autograph. Looking back, I realize that's as funny as a Mel Brooks movie, but I was terrified and very sick at the time. There can be humor in death, and dignity, too."

It still doesn't sound like a Burt Reynolds movie. "I hate to sound flip, but when you're one of the top five box-office money-makers for six straight years, you get power. I could go in and say I wanted to play a pink flamingo tap-dancing in feathers and they'd say, 'What can you bring it in for?' I did it because I wanted to stretch myself as an actor. Up to now, the directors I want to work with—Kubrick, Kazan, Coppola, et cetera—don't want to work with me. I decided a long time ago there were two ways I could go. One, like my friend Jon Voight, who doesn't work for five years at a time while he holds out for a paraplegic role with Jane Fonda. That would drive me crazy. Or, I could go my way. I said, dammit, I'll go for the power. I'll get so big they'll have to come to me.

"My whole career has been very carefully planned. I put on my 'Tonight' show face and it's a character I play. I see myself on TV and I think, 'Who is that flip, cocky, arrogant bastard?' But it worked. I became Phyllis Newman. And that personality caught on with the public and gave me the power to become a movie star.

"For years every time I did an interview or went on TV, I went into a telephone booth and changed into my Burt Reynolds outfit. My whole career's been very calculated. Posing nude for *Cosmopolitan* was calculated. I wouldn't do that now, but when I first started being noticed, I realized I'd have to develop a character the public would buy. When they started adding up the box-office receipts, they couldn't ignore me. I couldn't come to New York a year ago and talk to critics. I'd try to be cute and funny and we'd end up hating each other.

"I made rotten movies but the public bought 'em. I became sort of critic-proof. And I got the power, and it's fun. But at the same time I got no artistic rewards. What happened is that I got so good at playing 'good ol' boys' that people just think I'm playing myself. That character in *Smokey and the Bandit* is not the kind of role I want to play for the people I really care about."

The inner conflict between what he starved for artistically and what he was selling the unwashed masses peaked last year when he turned in his best performance since *Deliverance* in the Michael Ritchie football comedy *Semi-Tough*. "I got a collection of reviews that was staggering but nobody even wanted to know I was alive when it came time for Oscar nominations. So that's when I knew I'd either have to get a tracheotomy like Liz Taylor or play a guy with no legs.

"If it's respect I want inside this well-protected movie-star image, I'll have to become a real actor. To get back what I want for all the effort I've put out, I'll just have to give myself totally to one of these directors. So I'm literally wooing them. It would be to their credit, too, because if ever there was a star ready to burst, it's me. And the director who gets that performance out of Burt Reynolds will get the credit for being a genius."

He worships Elia Kazan, says he'd do "anything for him—*anything*!" Yet when he met the famous director he was downright rude. Kazan said, "I can't get over how much you look like Marlon Brando," and Reynolds said, "Oh, yeah? Well, you look like Harpo Marx!" He was, by his own admission, "an idiot and a snob" in those days. He feuded with *People* magazine, went on the "Today" show and when Barbara Walters asked him why he didn't marry Dinah Shore, he countered with "Why did you get a divorce?" He was insulting and insufferable. "I used to go out swinging. But I won't back away now. I decided to meet you today and be open, honest and see what happens. I'm ready to be vulnerable."

It's a cliché, but here is a case of a tough guy who needs to be loved. Faceless millions love the wrong guy. Beneath that honcho, chauvinist-pig, love-'em-and-leave-'em movie image beats the heart of a pussycat. He's been injured in the past and is still licking the wounds.

"For twenty years, I've waited for a director to put his arm around me and say, 'Let's talk about you!' It's never happened once. The only time a director put his arm around me, he walked me over to the edge of the set to tell me he needed one more shot before the sun went down. I tried to do a Broadway play once, a wonderful play called *Look, We've Come Through*. Every day José Quintero, the director, would come to rehearsal and hug everybody except me. I needed approval desperately, but they considered me a 'Hollywood actor.' Every day the cast would go off to lunch together, and I'd wander around by myself on the streets of New York, looking for somebody to eat with. It was a very painful experience.

"I went to California and played a blacksmith for two years on the 'Rawhide' TV series and Universal brought Clint Eastwood and me into the office and fired us. They told Clint his Adam's apple stuck out too far and he talked too slow. I said, 'What about me?' and they said, 'Well, you—you're just boring!' I made up my mind never to be boring again."

He married actress Judy Carne because "she was the first woman who ever thought I was witty." When he divorced her two years later, he called his mother to tell her. "We never hugged and kissed when I was a kid and I desperately wanted my father to tell me I was a man, but I told my mother to tell him I was getting a divorce. I said, 'Tell him he's right about me—I quit college, I quit New York, I quit 'Gunsmoke,' now I'm quitting my marriage.'

"My father got on the phone and said, 'Come home and I'll tell you about all the times I've failed in my life!' I flew down to Florida and we sat in the backyard and drank a bottle of cognac and got very drunk, and he told me some very touching stories about his own failures and I started to cry. Then he started to cry. I said, 'I've been cheated—hit me if you want to, but every time I see you from now on, I'm going to kiss you,' and now we're embarrassing. In essence, it was my father's way of telling me I was a man."

Hence, a new Burt Reynolds. Despite the image, he hates drinking beer and telling football stories. He reads a book a week. He's soft-spoken and warmly affectionate. His friends say he's fiercely loyal. He says Dinah Shore is still his best friend. He never goes to Hollywood parties, prefers to stay home and play charades. He does his own cooking. And only occasionally does the old arrogance flash through the pastels of his privacy.

"I trusted that director on *The End* more than any director I've ever worked with," he says defiantly.

The director of *The End* was Burt Reynolds.

5

MARTHE KELLER

FOR SOMEONE WHO IS SUDDENLY THE GIRL OF THE YEAR IN AMERICAN movies, Swiss-born Marthe Keller is being positively Garboesque about it. At a crucial career point when most girls would be dancing their buns off nightly for the paparazzi, she avoids publicity, doesn't do interviews, never goes to parties or restaurants, and hates Hollywood. Two years ago she couldn't speak one word of English. Now, after starring with Dustin Hoffman and Laurence Olivier in *Marathon Man,* she's going to be even bigger in *Black Sunday* and *Bobby Deerfield* (co-starring her own man of the hour, Al Pacino). That's three films in two years when most American actresses can't even get hired for one. "I'm an actress," she insists in her charming German accent. "I don't give a damn about being a movie star."

Shunning the sunshine and kidney-shaped pools of California, she's moved into a rented New York apartment with her six-year-old son, Alexander, where she can be even more anonymous. After some persuasion, she agrees to meet me there for four-o'clock tea. She opens the door herself because she has no maid, employs no servant, is without even a cook or nanny. On-screen, she's square-jawed, tough, an odd choice for girl of the year. In person, she's soft, feminine, almost lyrically beautiful. She makes apologies for the apartment, saying it belongs to somebody else, but the German influence is everywhere—a program from a Lotte Lenya-Kurt Weill museum exhibit, a collection of Marlene Dietrich advice to the lovelorn, records of Wagner operas, a book on the films of Billy Wilder. She makes tea, serves Pepperidge Farm chocolate-chip cookies, and becomes instantly adorable. "I don't do interviews, so when I finally agree to do one I like to make the most of it. With me, it's honest talk or nothing. I'm a woman of extremes. I either tell you everything or I shut up. I'm no good at small talk. The Hollywood life for me was a nightmare. I never go out. Once I went to dinner with my good friend John Schlesinger, who directed me in *Marathon Man*, and the German newspapers printed that I was his mistress!" She roars with laughter at the ridiculous thought. "So I was not very popular in Los Angeles. I never went to parties because they are so boring. Second, everybody says, 'How are you?' but nobody waits for an answer because they really don't care how you are. It's a waste of time. They always judge you—'Did you see how she looked today?' and 'Oh, my God, what did you do to your hair?'—and I couldn't take it."

The gossip she hated most was the juicy rumor that she got both *Marathon Man* and *Black Sunday* because she was the girlfriend of Robert Evans, who produced both films. "Jesus Christ, this is so depressing! You don't get a part by going to bed with a producer! There are girls ten times more beautiful than me, so I don't think I would get a part because of a superficial reason like looks. I never got a job through anyone I dated, but the honest truth is that I never had one date with Bob Evans. These rumors are idiotic! I was onstage in more than fifty roles for six years and made twelve films in Europe before *Marathon Man*. The truth is that Michael York and Dirk Bogarde saw me onstage in Paris in *Joe Egg* and when John Schlesinger was looking for a European actress for *Marathon Man* they both recommended me and he came to Paris to see me and asked me to do a test in Hollywood so he could see how I looked on the screen with Dustin Hoffman. That's when I met Bob Evans, so he didn't discover me at all! The idea of such a thing makes me furious."

The rumors got fanned even more when Evans used her in *Black Sunday*, in which she plays a Palestinian terrorist who plots the destruction of 82,000 innocent Americans at a Super Bowl game for pro-Arab political reasons. "But," she says, "the truth is that I turned down the film for two months because I didn't like the part. I was homesick for Europe, and for personal reasons I felt more close to Israel than Palestine and the role was very tough and I felt no sympathy for it. Also, I felt that part was too big a responsibility for someone who couldn't speak the English language properly. So I said no. The thing that changed my mind happened on a Friday afternoon. I took my child to see *Snow White* and in the middle of the movie he said, 'You know, Mommy, I prefer the bad lady—I really don't like Snow White too much!' So I called Paramount and said what the hell, I'll play a bad lady for a change—it's more interesting! That's the real reason. Now that movies cost ten million dollars you can't just hire your girlfriend to carry them. Those days are over. If I was a model who just got a starring role, I might understand those rumors, but I've been acting all my life. I don't have to prove I can act."

As if on cue, the door opens and in saunters Al Pacino, who is even shyer about interviews than Marthe. Does he turn white at the sight of my tape recorder? Does he flee in anger, shouting obscenities? Not a bit of it. He joins in, launching cheerfully into a discussion of his new play, the agonies of opening-night tension, and when Marthe says, "You see, you do give interviews!" he blushes, makes excuses and leaves politely for rehearsal, telling her he'll be home in time for dinner. Now all the cats are out of the bag. Marthe does not live alone. They are happy roommates. "Now I guess they'll say I got the starring role in Al's movie *Bobby Deerfield* because I'm living with him. Again the gossip starts. The truth"—she shrugs—"is that I didn't even know him when I started the film. I didn't live with him until the movie was finished. Now we've been together a year already, and they are just beginning to say I got the part because of Al. This is the part I hate about being an actress. I can't stand the drivers, the hairdressers, the interviews—it makes me feel vulgar. The truth"—she shrugs again—"is that when I fall in love in my life, it's when I see men work. I don't fall in love in a bar, I don't meet men in nightclubs, I don't take subways—I don't go anywhere to meet men except when I work, and that's when all of my romances begin. Then I fall for their talent and energy, not their faces. It's everything or nothing with me. I told you I'm a woman of extremes."

She admits to only two men in her life before Pacino—French director Philippe de Broca, who is the father of her son, then French director Claude Lelouch, who directed her in *And Now My Love*. She's still friendly with them both. "I always fall in love with a man's work first. I didn't want to marry De Broca. I do what I want to do. I live my life my way. I will not pay a price to be an actress. I raise Alex myself. I have no nurse, no nanny, nobody. I get up every morning at seven, take Alex to school at eight-thirty, then I pick him up at five-fifteen. I do not send chauffeurs for him. Come with me, you will see."

We pile into a taxi and head for Alex's school on East Seventy-ninth Street. On the way, she gives New York a rave review. "I was here many times, but you can't judge a city if you're living in a hotel. I feel very European here because everybody is from somewhere else. I took four cabs today, and the cab drivers were German, Italian, English and French—so I never felt alone because I could speak all four languages! People don't judge you in New York. You can have a private life. I don't get mobbed in the street like I do in Rome. I hope I can stay here and do a play, and I'm already talking to producers about being in either a revival of *A Month in the Country* or playing Joan of Arc in *The Lark*. I would like to have a career here and be taken seriously as an actress without all the Hollywood nonsense."

At the school, Alex tumbles out, clutching his blue Peanuts lunch box and babbling furiously in French. The language barrier means nothing to him. His teacher is Chinese, his classmates are from everywhere, and kids have a language all their own anyway. His English is improving, like his mom's, but they speak to each other only in French. Alex leads the way, like a Raggedy Andy doll gone berserk, to a Madison Avenue coffee shop, where he says, "Hello, how are you?" to everyone at the counter before collapsing into a chocolate sundae. "One year ago," says Marthe, "I couldn't say one word in English, but I took the role in *Marathon Man* just to work with Dustin Hoffman and Laurence Olivier in an American film. I hate school, so I didn't take courses. I learned from watching television and going to movies night and day. Then I bought a French magazine like *Newsweek* and compared all the stories in French about Jimmy Carter to the same stories in *Newsweek* and worked out my own translations. I'm completely self-taught. When I arrived in Paris from Germany, I couldn't speak French, either. Nine months later, I was starring in *Joe Egg* onstage. You can do anything if you try."

She's worried about her image, playing an unsympathetic villain in *Black Sunday,* but says, "It was an Arab terrorist or nothing. I did it to keep my career going, and I'm glad because it led to the role with Al in *Bobby Deerfield,* and that is my favorite part." She plays a vital, funny, spirited girl, dying of cancer, who falls in love with an American racing-car driver.

So many good parts during a dry spell for women must raise the ire of other actresses, but Marthe says she hasn't felt their animosity yet. "I don't go out, I don't see them. Frankly, I don't know any other actresses." She says she plans to remain a private person, but with so much exposure on film it won't be long before the fans come out of the woodwork. "Already," she sighs, "I get the crazy people who write and ask me to send them water from Lourdes."

She remains adamant about not doing interviews, insisting this is a rare one. "For Al, it's publicity not to make publicity. For me, it's no big deal. I just prefer to work. Working is the best publicity. You make a striptease for journalists, you don't know the people you are talking to, then they go away rich and you are left with nothing. Who needs it? I know actors who go to the right parties, get photographed all the time, and tell the press lies to make good stories, but they don't *work*! Me, I prefer to work. When I don't work, I do my own housework, my own cooking, and I never go out at night." Her publicist says she had to promise Marthe a baby-sitter before she would even go out to be photographed by Richard Avedon. In May, she'll be on the jury at the Cannes Film Festival ("Who is this girl Pauline Kael?" she asks innocently) and already she's announced she will not attend any time-wasting parties or social events. If she succeeds, she'll be the first actress who ever went to Cannes avoiding the flashbulbs instead of seeking them.

"I do what I want and answer to nobody." She smiles defiantly, scooping up her son in time to cook him his six-o'clock dinner. "I've always done everything alone and I plan to maintain my privacy and independence at all costs." She might get her wish. In the Madison Avenue traffic, she wiped chocolate ice cream from Alex's nose and in the slight bilingual rebellion that followed, Marthe Keller was no longer the girl of the year, capable of promising a great performance. She was just another mother, capable of promising a great spanking.

6

RICHARD GERE

RICHARD GERE. IF THE NAME DOESN'T EXACTLY STOP THE DOORMAN at Sardi's in his tracks, just wait. The doorman at Sardi's has a lot to learn. Millions are already swooning over his electrifying portrayal of Tony, the crazy, doped-up hustler you love to hate in *Looking for Mr. Goodbar*. In Hollywood, where a star is born every six weeks, Richard Gere is suddenly as hot as John Travolta, with four major movies under his belt and more offers than a math major can add up on a pocket tabulator. The odd thing is that Richard Gere hasn't done a thing to blow his own horn. Everyone else has been too busy doing it for him. If ever there was a brand-new movie star working overtime trying to convince everyone he's not a brand-new movie star, it's this elusive iconoclast.

This is his first interview. He turns up at his agent's office nervous as a first offender awaiting the jury. He's wearing faded blue jeans, a torn T-shirt ("I've had it since high school") and holes in the soles of his shoes. He rubs his forehead, squints his eyes, and seems on the verge of a terminal headache. He is deeply intense, like someone auditioning for Lee Strasberg. We can't meet at his New York apartment because he lives in an abandoned storefront near Westbeth and people are always peering through the glass to get a look at the movie star in its cage. No Malibu beach house or Beverly Hills mansion with kidney-shaped swimming pool? "Are you kidding, man? I'm just a neighborhood punk. The storefront has been home for the last five years. I was only broken into once. It's safe, you know, a lot of Spanish families, a lot of longshoremen. They've just discovered me. They don't see *Goodbar*. Those people don't go to movies. Somebody tells them. I could be anything—a politician or a pimp. Your name and your picture get in the paper and they start giggling. It was a plumber's store before I moved in. It's the size of one of those Puerto Rican groceries. It's ten feet wide and about thirty feet long and it's divided into three rooms with two lofts and a fireplace. It's a gas. The problem is, there's no light. No sunlight. I have a big window on the street filled with plants. It's terrific after midnight. Before that, I lived in dumps in the far East Village. Sixth between Avenues C and D. They don't deliver mail there, the fire department doesn't even answer an alarm. Those were the tragic years."

It wasn't an overnight success. He's twenty-eight and he's been on his own since he was eighteen. He grew up in Syracuse, one of five children born to a family of farmers. "My family never goes to films, but they saw *Goodbar*. They're very unsophisticated people. My father sells insurance now, my mother is a housewife. One brother, three sisters. None of them are in show business, but they're all eccentric." He was a small-town kid, but he had images in his head growing up "of punks, motorcycles, leather jackets, knives, violence, the whole obvious James Dean-Brando bit. It seems like I've been doing punks ever since." He majored in philosophy at the University of Massachusetts, dropped out after two years, got a summer-stock job in Provincetown, played roles at the Seattle Rep, dropped out of acting to join a rock group living on an old farm in Vermont. "I played guitar and keyboards. It was about three hundred acres of land on top of a mountain. Trout streams, the whole thing. But then we didn't get along. Musicians are even harder to get along with than actors."

He wandered down to New York, got the first job he auditioned for, in a rock opera called *Soon*. The shock to his nervous system began with early success. "It took me two years just to get used to New York. Every day I found myself on the railing of the East River trying not to jump in. I came here knowing nobody. The only person

I knew in New York was an old girlfriend who didn't want to know I was alive, man." He did *Grease* in London, *Habeas Corpus* on Broadway. Then the bizarre roles started happening. He was a pimp in *Report to the Commissioner* and a shell-shocked albino killer in *Baby Blue Marine*. The word was out: here is this phenomenally talented, gorgeous new maniac who plays crazy lunatic punks, has guitar, will travel. He fled to Canada, moved heaven and earth to get the lead in Terence (*Badlands*) Malick's film *Days of Heaven*, which is still unreleased but which insiders say is one of the knockout films of the forthcoming season. "It's a 1916 period piece. I play a John Garfield punk steelworker from Chicago who runs away from the cops with his girlfriend and younger sister and gets lost in the wheat harvest down South. It's about people trying to find some sunshine and some peace in their lives. If it had been released before *Looking for Mr. Goodbar* people might have a different image of me now," he says ruefully.

He had finished the picture, was on his way back to his storefront in New York, when he got a call from Paramount saying they couldn't find the right guy to play Tony the hustler who terrorizes Diane Keaton in the Richard Brooks movie. "I didn't know anything about *Goodbar*. I thought it was just some cheap piece of crap novel. But I decided to talk to them. I met Richard Brooks. Literally, I just walked in and took the part. There wasn't much film on me. Brooks just took me on reputation. He didn't want to futz around spoon-feeding some actor who didn't know when to hit his marks. I told him I wanted to read the script, so what he did was go through the script, and just show me my lines. If my line started in the middle of a page, he'd rip off the top of the page, so I couldn't read any of the other actors' lines. He's a wild director, man. But after the first day of shooting, he trusted me totally. He knew I understood the character as well as he did, and I got total support. Knowing Tony wasn't the real killer made it easy to be as ugly or as outrageous as I wanted to be because I knew the audience would end up loving me. I'm not aggressive in real life. I'm very shy. Diane Keaton was shy, too. She was very nervous about the sex scenes. I was nervous about everything. I walked into a film that was already shooting and I didn't know anybody. Because of my own insecurity, I was very uptight the first day and she thought I didn't like her or respond to her as an actress, but we worked out our problems and it was a very creative experience. The set was closed, we improvised a lot. Brooks was right there, concentrating his energy on ours, so he was like an alter ego for us. Brooks was the best experience I've ever had. He told me no more than I needed and made me feel supremely confident. There was never any doubt in my mind that here was an incredible human being, working from a very clean place, with no dollar motive at all. He totally changed my ideas about filmmaking."

Looking for Mr. Goodbar was really threatening and upsetting to millions of viewers. Richard Brooks's life was threatened and his home vandalized. Now Gere is getting the feedback. "People bug me, nuts call me up in the middle of the night. They're cooler about it in New York, but they still expect me to be a punk. I think the critics would have liked the film better if it had starred anyone other than Diane Keaton. People have so many preconceived ideas about her that they felt she was violated by the film, therefore they were violated by the film." It made Richard Gere what the folks in the trade call "a hot property," but he refused to strike when the iron was still steaming. "I talked to nobody. I refused to do publicity interviews. Things moved so fast I felt like the Flavor of the Month. I just couldn't take it. Even now I could walk away from the whole thing."

He still sees himself as "an actor with an Off Broadway mentality" surrounded by the January white sales of success talk. "Offers are pouring in, people are talking about percentages, grosses, development deals, director approval. It's too much for me to deal with. I'm trying to keep my own soul together. I don't want to get an image that won't allow me to change and grow. I don't want my privacy projected upon by the public." To change the punk image, he went instantly into Robert Mulligan's *Bloodbrothers*, about a tightly knit family of Italian construction workers in the Bronx. "I play the sensitive hard-hat son trying to get out. Next, I'm doing John Schlesinger's movie *Yanks*, about three American soldiers in love with English girls before D-Day. That'll show the world the all-American Richard Gere. I'll have to get a short haircut. I'm trying to be different each time. You wanna know how success has changed me? When you start out acting, you just want to work. You're not concerned with the messages of the pieces or the motives of the people making them. As I've been given more responsibility in a medium that is seen by millions and has a tremendous influence on the psyche of the world, I find myself choosing projects that are something I can believe in morally. In one year, I've worked for Malick, Brooks, Mulligan and Schlesinger. I doubt if I'll ever have another year that enriching."

Is he rich? "Are you kidding? I've made nothing, man. Until I got the Schlesinger film, I was still on unemployment. Material things—cars, houses, a fast lifestyle—mean nothing to me. From now on, I'm taking the bread I make and investing it in scripts I want to develop on my own. It's hard to convince people in Hollywood an actor can do other things. If you're an actor who plays punks, they don't expect you to come in with your own project. They're starting to understand me now, because I have turned down so many films in the last six months they're beginning to realize 'Hey, this guy's about something else besides being a movie star.' Most of my ideas are too esoteric for Hollywood. I mean, I like Herzog and Fassbinder. Too far out. They only understand dollars and cents in Hollywood. I sent a lot of people out there to see *The Mystery of Kasper Hauser* and it left them cold because it didn't have a plot. I think my ideas are so much better than everyone else's. I see no reason why I can't make personal films like the Germans. The only answer is to keep making viable commercial films with good directors and hope my so-called Hollywood name will make me a good enough financial risk to make films like Herzog on my own."

For the past six years, he's been living with actress Penelope Milford, who played the silent-screen star who seduced Nureyev to prove he wasn't gay in *Valentino*. "A crap movie, but she was good in it," he says. "She's pretty eccentric." He's never been married. He was in analysis once. "I'm still screwed up, but who isn't?" He must be doing something right. If the doorman at Sardi's doesn't know him yet, the customers do.

John Travolta

Fred Zinnemann and Vanessa Redgrave

Geraldine Fitzgerald

Burt Reynolds

Marthe Keller

Richard Gere

Sophia Loren and Carlo Ponti

PHOTO © TAZIO SECCHIAROLI/SYGMA

Jack Lemmon MARTHA SWOPE

7

SOPHIA LOREN

ST. LUCIA. THIRTEEN MILES FROM THE EQUATOR, SOPHIA LOREN IS melting. Because of a four-hour stall in Martinique, my plane doesn't land in the sun-kissed, bug-infested paradise called St. Lucia until 6:30 P.M. Sophia has gone to bed, exhausted from the heat, leaving the press agent on her new film *Firepower* to explain the plot. It's an eight-million-dollar mystery-thriller, directed by England's wild and woolly Michael Winner, about an illegal attempt by the U. S. Government to force back to America a billionaire financier wanted for fraud, tax evasion and other crimes for which he can't be extradited. Sophia plays "a mysterious adventuress," and that's all anybody's telling. James Coburn, O. J. Simpson, George Grizzard and Anthony Franciosa are her co-stars. They've already spent four weeks filming in Antigua and will travel on to Curaçao before finishing in New York, Washington and Miami.

Italy's greatest invention since fettucine Alfredo might have flaked out early, but at the tropical village they call the La Toc Hotel, George Grizzard is sipping piña coladas while the hibiscus turns magenta in the humid night. Asked how he's enjoying this vacation from the air-conditioned Broadway stage, he grins impishly. "Seven weeks in the Caribbean with Sophia Loren, it's tough, really tough!" Indeed he looks relaxed and tan, wearing his tropical Arthur Godfrey shirt out in island fashion. "For the last two days I've spent hours hanging from a helicopter with one foot, machine-gunning O. J. Simpson in a boat, and I'm scared to death of guns. It's a far cry from running up and down the stairs in a smoking jacket in *The Royal Family*. But I still can't believe I'm working in a movie with Sophia. She's fantastic!" What kind of character is he playing? "I'm evil, but sophisticated, what else? Next week we film my devastating death scene in boiling, burning water. I so hope Michael Winner will let me watch it—from a hill. This is one scene where they better use a stunt man. Film work is terrific because there's something new every day, you work for seven weeks, and it's finished. Long runs in a play are becoming increasingly more difficult. Today I had the whole day off. I rested, read *Letters from Virginia Woolf*, played cricket, and worried about planting vegetables on my Connecticut farm. I won't get home until so late in the season I might not have tomatoes until December! I just bought a machete for two dollars to cut my grass, which will be four feet high." Then he ponders. "How am I going to wrap a machete for the plane trip home?"

8:30 A.M. In the sleepy town of Soufrière, the pier is crowded with cameras, sound equipment, lights and fifty technicians. Winner, who directed *Death Wish, The Sentinel* and most recently the roundly roasted *Big Sleep*, disembarks from a yacht with his male stars. Grizzard has asked what the news is on Broadway, but Jim Coburn and O. J. Simpson want to know what's happening on the sports pages. Distance from civilization has fried their brains. Winner wears a towel around his neck, plus numerous viewfinders. "Sophia is changing, but will be here shortly." Coburn, fresh from TV's "Dain Curse," plays his flute while Winner teases treetop-tall O.J. "You got a two for piloting the boat yesterday, think you could try for a seven today?" "You turkey," counters Simpson, "I was great!" Winner's description of blowing up a yacht for one of the action scenes is interrupted by the clatter of birds and a frenzied croaking of crickets. Something is in the wind, and it's not bay rum. All heads turn to the pier and there she is. Wearing a pale-green halter dress that looks sprayed on, walking the unmistakable anchovy walk. She starts oozing her way toward us. She is glorious, she is—well, Sophia! Can it be twenty-one years since she climbed aboard Alan Ladd's boat soaking wet in *Boy on a Dolphin* to make movie history? Time has fallen in love with Sophia Loren.

Winner breaks the hypnosis: "She's so professional. The cast has been besieged by bugs, mice, bats, mongeese and paparazzi—but she never complains. She works six days and sleeps on Sunday. O.J. screamed like a twelve-year-old when a grasshopper fell on him, but you don't get a peep out of Sophia. The first day on the boat the sea was very rough and the yacht terribly crowded, she worked until eleven A.M. and then was violently seasick. But at eleven thirty she was back for her close-ups." She heads for her chair, which like the director's is the size of a throne compared to the deck chairs with the other players' names on them. There's even a sensuality to the way she sits, lifting her skirt and crossing her long legs. She cups her chin with one hand and chain-smokes with the other. She is constantly protected from the sun's burning rays by a large rainbow-colored beach umbrella. She applies her own makeup, while a flunky busies herself tidying that independent Loren mane. Where else but in the movies would any fool try to improve perfection?

During setups, O. J. Simpson plops down in Winner's chair ("It's a cardinal sin to sit in the director's chair, but I feel like sinning") and breaks up the cast and crew by telling terrible riddles and doing a coin trick, using Jim Coburn as his accomplice. Everyone connected with *Firepower* seems to be having a fling. Coburn, playing a bounty hunter, attributes his calm demeanor to yoga and Zen. Simpson's enthusiasm for acting equals his passion for football. "Michael, when can I see the rushes?" he teases. "I want to see if my eyebrows are moving too much." "They don't move when you talk, only when you act," Winner retorts. He and O.J. are like a comedy duo, constantly exchanging barbs and insults, plus a running commentary on who had the most famous alumni from their respective alma maters. "George Cukor went to USC," challenges O.J. Winner counters with "Robert Browning." O.J. even chides the stoic Sophia into joining the game. "Yes, many famous people come from Italy, too," she says seriously. "Yeah," grins O.J., "like Luciana Paluzzi!" Everyone breaks up, and Winner assembles his merry group for the next shot.

It's a day-for-night shot, so the headlights on a car must be adjusted to appear brighter through a filter. Coburn and O.J. come barreling down the pier as Sophia's dress blows slightly in the breeze. "Cut! Good shot, Sophia, but O.J.'s eyebrows were moving!" Now it is noon. Hundreds of children in blue uniforms descend from a convent school with reggae music blaring from their portable radios. In a nearby cathedral, thirteen-year-olds sell pot while a black Christ glares ominously from an altar covered with plastic flowers. Food is served by a caterer who once fed 17,000 Bolivian soldiers on the set of Harold Robbins' *The Adventurers.*

Night. Dinner with Michael Winner at a fantastic restaurant called Rain. Hanging flowers, powerful drinks called the Reverend's Downfall, and a local St. Lucia fish called *accra.* In the blue night, Winner looks like a younger, thinner, cuddlier Peter Ustinov. He's having a ball directing this whodunit because it has "tongue-in-cheek elements, many major plot twists, plus lots of surprises," he says, adding "there are nine thousand different shots I must personally edit into small pieces, mammoth action scenes, a jigsaw puzzle of immense proportions. I've done all of my films on location, but I've had ludicrous problems with this one. Six court cases are pending in Antigua for damages I had nothing to do with. Thank God for Sophia. She and Marlon Brando are the best artists I've ever directed. They know what everyone on the set is doing, and they comment with their eyes, which miss nothing and tell all."

8 A.M. Another harbor, at Anse-la-Raye. Sophia is wearing tight jeans, a see-through peasant blouse, and it is quite evident she is braless. (You'll see more of her in *Firepower* than Carlo Ponti does.) O.J. is beating her at gin rummy. She rolls her almond eyes skyward each time he yells "Gin." Winner calls places and she does "that walk" to the pier while a chicken strolls across the dirt courtyard, pecks at the remains of her cigarette, the only unimpressed creature on the island. Over lunch in a very hot makeshift commissary, Sophia sighs: "So much beautiful scenery, but I can't visit the tourist attractions as I'm so tired at the end of the day from the heat, wind and humidity, I go to bed after cooking some pasta I have flown in from London. Then I'm up at five A.M. and prepare Italian coffee with my own special little machine." She bums another cigarette. The flame from my lighter almost barbecues that beatific nose. She does the Sophia giggle. She wears a short dime-store robe and her head is filled with pin curlers, yet she is still every inch the Vesuvius she appears on the screen. She talks incessantly about her children. No, she has no intention of living in America to escape the kidnapping threats, although her dream is to do a Broadway musical.

"I have never had applause from a paying audience," she says wryly. She absolutely refuses to discuss her forthcoming trial in Italy, where she and Carlo Ponti have been accused of exporting money. In fact, when she finishes *Firepower* she plans to return to her homeland to star in Lina Wertmuller's next film. Never, never does she speak of retiring from the screen. (She's only forty-three and, like Brie, improving with age.) "I will never announce my plans in public, like some other people." She sniffs. "If I decide to quit, I will just tiptoe out quietly the way I came in."

8 P.M. Anthony Franciosa has just arrived to play the personal physician to the mysterious billionaire. He is so nervous you'd think he had never seen a movie camera before. Never mind the fact that he's Italian, too, or that he was once married to Shelley Winters. He's trim, tan and for the first time in his career he's grown a beard that shows his age. The beard is white and so is the X ray of his nervous stomach. "I'm so terribly excited about working with Sophia Loren I can hardly talk," he babbles. Michael Winner drops by the table to ask if anyone has seen Franciosa. He doesn't recognize him with the beard. Will we recognize him on the screen? The suspense is killing.

6 A.M. The car is leaving for the airport. Pigs sleep in the road, barefoot women haul their laundry on their heads, and miles of banana trees are being wrapped in huge blue Baggies to protect them from insects. Birds scream, Jim Coburn plays his flute on the beach at dawn, and Sophia does "that walk" for the last time, on her way to work. On the road, the car is confronted by a group of shouting natives with their fists raised high. Panic sets in, then fades into laughter when I realize they are chanting: "Sophia Loren, Firepower!" She waves, rolls her eyes to the cobalt sky, then disappears. Heigh-ho, the glamorous life.

8

JACK LEMMON

BOSTON. THE SCREAMING JITTERS, THE FRYING NERVES, THE "How did I ever get into this?" blues that usually plague Broadway shows trying out in Boston are refreshingly absent from the backstage cheerfulness surrounding Jack Lemmon in *Tribute*. The play hits New York June 1, but Jack Lemmon's nails aren't bitten to the quick. The audience has just given him a standing ovation, and when he slips into a booth in the Ritz-Carlton bar, freshly shaven and gentle as cashmere, his hand doesn't shake when he downs his first Bloody Mary of the day.

"I'm cautious, but I'm not hysterical," he says, lighting up a new cigar. "To tell you the truth, everybody is so sure we've got a hit that I'd like to see a few more nerves. I think we're right on the edge of a hell of a play."

The play was written by Bernard Slade, whose *Same Time, Next Year* is one of the comedy blockbusters of this decade. Lemmon plays a press agent dying of leukemia who tries to clean up the mess he's made of his relationships with his son, friends and ex-wife before he kicks the bucket. It's a nonstop, marathon, pull-out-the-stops, full-steam-ahead role, and he's just plain fabulous.

"It's awfully difficult to make the audience laugh and cry at the same time," he says, "and that's why I wanted to play this character. I didn't know how to play him and that's what grabbed me. Usually, if you know how to play a role, then you've already played it. This play has comedy and drama combined and the last time I found a script like that was *The Apartment*. This guy has a touch of class. He drops his pants and he wears a chicken suit but he has some dignity, too, and I just kind of fell in love with this play. I've had to restructure my life to do it."

The last time Jack Lemmon starred on Broadway was eighteen years ago, in *Face of a Hero* with Sandy Dennis. "It was lousy. The more we worked on it, the worse it got. I learned discipline, but it was like beating a dead horse. And I've been offered a lot of plays in the eighteen years since, but nothing excited me as much as *Tribute*. Bernie Slade wrote the play for me and sent it to me from Canada in a brown garbage bag all crumpled up with string around it. I thought it was garbage. I didn't know what the hell it was. It had a note attached that said, 'I wrote this with you in mind so I might as well send it to you.' I read it. Flipped. I was looking for a play, it just sort of happened. Right away, bang. The deal was set in three days."

He had to uproot the family, move everybody to the East Coast, turn down a lot of money and percentages in films. "You just have to be prepared to say, 'Well, I lost *Ben-Hur*' or something. But this is more important to me as an actor and, no matter what happens, I'll never regret it. I feel marvelous, even though I'm exhausted."

The play is not about Jack Lemmon, but based on a real-life character named Harvey Orkin, "sort of an Ernie Kovacs nut who was a very witty, charming, delightful guy. He was a press agent, he was an actors' agent, he did a lot of things on the fringe of show business. He used to handle Richard Burton and Elizabeth Taylor. One night his clients didn't show up to do a David Frost show in London, so Harvey went on instead and became a star.

"He was on every week. He was one of the great practical jokers. He'd get international operators so screwed up they'd go to pieces. He'd call up somebody overseas at the home of a friend and when the friend would say, 'I'm sorry, it's three o'clock in the morning in California, he's out,' Harvey would say, 'That's absolutely ridiculous, Operator, that man is a hopeless invalid, with no legs, so he couldn't possibly go anywhere, don't tell me he's out, Operator!' It got to the point where everybody in the world would break up when Harvey called.

"Well, Harvey woke up at fifty with leukemia. And his biggest problem was when he was in the hospital. He never had a moment's peace. Hundreds of people kept coming up to see him. He would sit there telling jokes while he was dying. He was the most popular SOB that ever walked. Bernie Slade knew him and that's how this play got started. Most of the stuff in it comes from Harvey Orkin, and we keep adding new stuff all the time."

There are parallels between the character in *Tribute* and Jack Lemmon. He's been "on" ever since he sang and danced in drag in the Hasty Pudding shows at Harvard (1946), he's been playing the piano since he was thirteen, and he had the generation-gap problem with his son Chris, twenty-three, from his first marriage to actress Cynthia Stone.

"We went through that whole teen-age syndrome of being on different wavelengths. He's pulled himself together now, though, and we're great friends. And it's very creepy because the boy who plays my son onstage looks just like Chris and sounds just like him, and sometimes I feel like I'm living my life onstage. It's creepy."

As for his own health, Jack is fine now, but was "sick as hell as a kid. I missed a year of school. Had major operations, time after time. I had three mastoid operations all before penicillin, had my adenoids out five times, tonsils three times, they just kept growing back and causing all sorts of respiratory problems. I still can't breathe out of both sides of my nose at the same time. And all the childhood diseases, they just kept piling on. So eventually I'd leave school every day at noon and they'd drive me to a gym and I'd work out and do some running and suddenly, at about age twelve, I guess they ran out of diseases or I had already had them all, but anyway, I have never really been seriously ill since. Only minor sinus problems."

He says the gossip-column reports of his heavy drinking are wild exaggerations. "They've made me an alcoholic since the time I did *Days of Wine and Roses*. I began to get thousands of letters of advice. Honest to God. And those damn things started to hit the papers and then I'd read that I'd been drunk at a party and holding a woman over an open flame. Oh, boy. I haven't fallen victim to any of those

Hollywood social diseases. My wife, Felicia, and I don't go out much. You can't work in films or perform in the theater if you're a drunk. You'd fall over if you weren't in shape. On film, you'd look like hell. There's no way to hide it when that camera moves in and your eye is three feet wide. I never tried to get plastered to make *Days of Wine and Roses* more realistic, either. Marlon Brando tried that on a picture, and they all went home. Couldn't get a single shot."

Like the man in *Tribute*, Jack says there was a time in his life when he felt the need to be the life of the party, "to feed an ego that couldn't be sated. But something happened to me when I passed forty. I just stopped caring what other people thought. I've never been to an analyst, but I can trace the decline of my concern with image. I just started accepting myself as a human being. I think I've come to terms with myself. The fear of failure is the worst thing in the world because it stops you from trying new things.

"When I did my last play in New York I came out of the biggest bomb that ever fell and nothing happened. There were a lot of film offers by noon the following day because when they read the notices they knew I was out of work. Sometimes failure is a healthy thing. Anyway, who the hell knows what will happen with this new play? The important thing is I am not playing it safe."

Does he have any limitations? "Yes. I've never been able to play cowboys or gladiators. Can you see me as Ben Hur? There is a hunk of film hidden away in a vault somewhere that Harry Cohn made me do for the lead in *Joseph and His Brothers*. I want to tell you that when I put on that little hopsack skirt with the baby booties laced up to my knees and a jockstrap and a wig, I looked like Geronimo's niece. I walked onto that set and the grips started falling out of the rafters. And I did the test under protest with Rita Hayworth. After the test, Harry Cohn not only hid the film on me, but he canceled the whole movie. For years, he said, 'If you ever give me any trouble, I'll show that film all over the Bel Air circuit.' I'd love to play the Dauphin in *Saint Joan* or Iago. I wish I had played Cyrano. But let's face it. There's something very contemporary about me. I look better on the golf course than in a Roman chariot."

He doesn't believe in competition among actors, says the Oscars he's won don't mean a thing, doesn't envy a single living soul. "I've done bombs I can't stand to look at on TV, but I've always taken chances. Every day I realize how much more there is to learn as an actor. I'm not satisfied with my work all the time, which is good. When you get complacent, you get stale.

"My father had a marvelous attitude. He was a baker and even after he retired he was still thinking up ways to bake a better doughnut. He'd go down the street and look at shops and think of ways to merchandise bread better. He was passionate about his life.

"From the time I was in knee pants, I wanted to be famous. I never dreamed of movies. It was always the stage. In my first movie with Judy Holliday, George Cukor drove me crazy. I'd come in every day with five thousand ideas, and he'd just say, 'Less, less, less, Jack. Less is more.' Ten days into the film, I thought I had an ulcer from worry. Finally, I blew up and yelled, "Are you trying to tell me *not* to act?' and he said, 'Oh, God, *yes*!' And I never forgot it.

"I've learned my craft from that advice. If you're thinking and planning it while you're doing it, then you're really not doing it. It's the hardest thing in the world to be simple and the easiest thing in the world to act your brains out and make an ass out of yourself. I've spent my life trying to get down to the basic truth without the frills, and I've had good working relationships with directors.

"Judy Holliday taught me that tranquillity is all-important if you want to get the work done. On *Some Like It Hot*, Tony Curtis hated Marilyn Monroe, but I never had a problem. It's been like that on all of my films, and when I die I hope they remember me with respect. If I have any regrets, it's only that I've never played a psychotic maniac killer and I'm still looking for a role like that, something truly evil. But whether I just keep on being 'good ol' Jack Lemmon' or not, I'll never know everything there is to know about my business. I've forgotten my lines onstage before, and I just start all over again and try it a different way, and that's how I've lived my life and that's why I'm here today, ready to give birth on Broadway."

Jack Lemmon is still looking for a better doughnut.

9

DOROTHY MCGUIRE

DOROTHY MCGUIRE. THE SIMPLE ACT OF REPEATING THE NAME aloud is an act of reassurance; there's something solid and comfortable in the sound.

For twenty years, she radiated kindness, warmth and understanding from the movie screen as one of Hollywood's most appealing leading ladies. With a voice like creamy melted cocoa, bordering on a soft whisper, and a gentle, unselfish femininity that spilled over into the floodlights and illuminated the dark corners of the screen around her, she was the living embodiment of Currier and Ives Christmases and plenty of tea and sympathy. She could never have been a Rita or a Lana. No, she had to be a Dorothy.

In recent years, when one has been lucky enough to catch a glimpse of her, she's been somebody's grandmother, or some old creature dying of something unfortunate in a string of Disneyish family epics. On last year's "Rich Man, Poor Man" she was the long-suffering mother of Nick Nolte and Peter Strauss, who ended up bitter and wretched after a lifetime of deprivation, but on her deathbed, that class shone through long enough to touch the heart. What a shock and a relief, then, to meet her face to face on Broadway, where she's returned after a lamentable absence of too many empty years once again to light up the sky in the current smash-hit revival of Tennessee Williams' *The Night of the Iguana*, and then in her own clothes and her own smile in her New York hotel suite.

One handshake and you know what opportunities the movies have missed. Dorothy McGuire is radiant and shining, in the prime of her years. While the movies criminally neglected her, she busied herself with a real and productive life built on more solid foundations. At fifty-seven, when most former screen idols are drowning their despair in alcohol and want ads, Dorothy McGuire is getting on with her life, rediscovering herself. There are no tears in her beer.

No, she says emphatically, she never retired. "I just didn't want to play monsters, and after a long list of rather distinguished roles, I just wasn't getting the kinds of scripts that interested me. I had my husband and my family and a very rewarding life at home, and I didn't feel the need to work when the work wasn't interesting or fulfilling, so I just waited. Now I consider myself enormously lucky to be in this beautiful play. It's very challenging, and I'm finding new layers to uncover each day. My whole career has been lucky to be able to give of myself over a period of time in one profession, raise two children and still hold everything together."

Survival is her middle name. So many actresses have used it to describe professional longevity that the word has almost been demoted to cliché status, but with McGuire it has fresh meaning. Very few women are as pulled together emotionally and professionally as she is. "Two words. John Swope." She smiles meltingly at her husband of thirty-three years, the famous photographer who sits nearby, intently scanning a book of photos he's taken over several decades in the most remote reaches of the universe for publications like *Life*. While his wife toils nightly at the Circle in the Square, evoking the poetic visions of a Nantucket spinster stranded in a seedy Mexican jungle in *Iguana*, Swope is preparing an exhibition and a forthcoming book.

"If you knew my husband better," says Dorothy, "you'd know how lucky I've been. I love my career but I never really thought much about how to nurture it. I had a strong marriage, a secure home to go home to, and we traveled a great deal. All of those things were terribly important. If I seem vague and evasive about my career, it's because I didn't think about it that heavily. If I ticked off all the places we've been while John was photographing the world—sometimes on assignment, sometimes on holiday—you'd see the advantages I've had. I've seen the most sophisticated life and the most primitive tribal life side by side, and it's helped me totally as an actress.

"I've always been rather shy and not very adventurous. But travel freed me. The young people today are not afraid. They plunge blindly into things. But I come from a slightly different period. My favorite quote for myself is that I can now travel light and fast and make tracks and light the way. I could never say that before." After *Iguana* closes, she won't rest on her laurels. She will be on the Trans-Siberian express to Russia, Persepolis, Japan and Samarkand. If Hollywood beckons, it'll have to be by cable.

Now in her middle years, she's finally getting to play roles with sexuality for the first time, both in *Iguana* and another recent production of *Sweet Bird of Youth* in Los Angeles. It's a side of her nobody discovered before. "I was always the good woman. I don't know to this day what shapes a career out in Hollywood. It's still rather mysterious. It has, I think, a lot to do with how you look, what's available, how you take off at the box office. Or sometimes they don't know how to use you, so you find yourself lost. I was never a classic beauty, I had no image, so I found myself in a lot of things accidentally, like *The Enchanted Cottage* and *A Tree Grows in Brooklyn* and *Gentleman's Agreement*, and they all worked to my advantage. I did make one picture called *Till the End of Time*, in which I played an older woman who seduced Guy Madison and everyone was shocked, and the film was a failure. Today, that is quite fashionable. I went right back into playing nice girls and faithful wives, which today wouldn't be considered very appealing. Movies have changed and women are looked at quite differently."

Didn't she ever want to say, "Look, fellas, I can be a lusty tart, too?"

"Not really. Looking back, I wasn't all that aware of what was happening. David Selznick saw me on Broadway in *Claudia* and brought me to Hollywood to do the film version in 1943. By that time I was married, and not very ambitious. It never occurred to me that I should direct my career in any direction. I just wanted to act." She always did. Like Marlon Brando, Henry Fonda, Dick Cavett and Sandy Dennis, she came from Nebraska, where she made her debut at thirteen when Fonda came home to Omaha and appeared with her in a community theater production. "I love young actors and their passion and I don't know how they ever make it today. In those days, it was simple. There wasn't the competition, the economic problem of how to live while waiting for a break, or the demand that you had the right training. Of course, luck plays an important part and I kicked off well.

"I went to a convent school, then a junior college, but it was all just marking time until I was eighteen and my father let me go to New York. I apprenticed in summer stock in Maine, lived at the undertaker's parlor, and worked in touring productions with fabulous stars, and it was just great. Today, it's much more difficult for young actors. There are no freeloaders. Jobs are scarce, inflation takes a big bite out of salaries, and salaries are low. I didn't have to struggle. I got a CBS radio job on a soap opera called 'Big Sister,' understudied Martha Scott in *Our Town*, and my greatest ambition was to get into a play the Theatre Guild did called *Liberty Jones*. Another actress got it, and I was sent instead to read for *Claudia*, which I didn't want to do." *Liberty Jones* ran for three weeks and *Claudia* ran for two years and made her a movie star.

She went from one memorable film to another—*Claudia, A Tree Grows in Brooklyn, Gentleman's Agreement, The Spiral Staircase, Invitation, Three Coins in the Fountain, Trial, Friendly Persuasion, The Dark at the Top of the Stairs.*

But even then her name seldom appeared in columns. You never read stories about her going to flashy parties or jumping into swimming pools. "I was never glamorous or beautiful and I considered myself a theater actress. There were never any scandals or drinking champagne out of slippers, or nude orgies. I suppose we drank our share of champagne, but I don't remember any slippers. If there were Hollywood orgies, they must have waited until John and I went home." Even today, the Swopes keep a low profile in the eye of the Hollywood needle. "We don't go to parties or premieres. We have an old circle of friends you don't read about in the headlines. We don't see much of that glamorous rock-and-roll scene."

It isn't surprising that she turned out more gentle and less neurotic than other stars her age. "I was never very competitive. If you were suddenly discovered and very beautiful and got paid fabulous sums of money, there's no reason why you should not be mixed-up in a business all exaggerated and out of proportion with reality to begin with. It's different when you come from the theater, where you lived in small dressing rooms and studied your craft and learned a humbling experience through hard work." Now her daughter, Topo Swope, twenty-seven, is an aspiring actress. Does her famous mother give advice? "No, I take it. She's much more tuned in to what's happening today than I am. You just have to have a strong, coping instinct and hang in there and keep going. That's what a career is about, if you love it. Look at my co-star in *Iguana,* Richard Chamberlain. He had a comfortable life on TV, but he developed his craft instead, took a very bold step, went to England and played Hamlet on their home ground, and he never stops perfecting his art. Now he has the equipment, intelligence and good looks to be the leading star of our theater today. He can go anywhere he wants with his career. I can't say enough about him or Joe Hardy, our director. They're the poets who put the magic into this play.

"I think the generation gap is closing. Topo called me once and said she'd been offered a movie role but it was topless and what did I think of that? I said, 'Topo, you're over twenty-one. I could answer for myself, but you'll have to make your own decision.' Later she said, 'I was longing for you to say yes or no, but you forced me to make up my own mind and I grew up a bit.' It's not easy for parents. They want you to know all the answers, but then they use them against you. We've tried to make our children understand that if you remove the labels, parents are just people twenty years older with the same problems and hangups they have. Kids today think we don't understand their era and in some respects they're right.

"We don't give them enough credit. They've been brave, they've explored, they've copped out and been lost. But they've made us aware. With their angers and their drugs and their desires to find new answers, they've awakened us sharply and been an enormous value. They've given us more plusses than losses. It's like existentialism—you never know what you had until the cup is broken. It's like that with a career. If you worry about billing and money and close-ups and how you look, you'll end up unfulfilled. I was never interested in any of those things and it's turned out all right. The most valuable advice I ever got was from Elia Kazan, who said, 'Don't tell me—show it, do it!' To this day I don't like to talk about acting—I just do it. Life is like that. If your priorities are right for you, you'll somehow come out all right. Listen," she closes wisely, "acting is rough. Life is rough. And if you're alone in either, it's even rougher. All I can say is, God bless us all."

10

GOLDIE HAWN

GOLDIE HAWN BREEZED INTO TOWN LAST WEEK LIKE THE FIRST crocus of spring. "I've changed," she said, munching a veal chop in her hotel room, and it didn't take much imagination to see why. Gone is the old Tweety Pie expression from "Laugh-In." She's ditched the teased hair and the dumb-blonde image, too. At the Academy Awards, she was one of the best-dressed and most dignified presenters onstage in the middle of what looked like a Hollywood junkyard. Goldie has grown up.

I hadn't seen her for two years. The last time, she was still married to fledgling director Gus Trikonis and very pregnant by Bill Hudson, a member of the Hudson Brothers rock group. Hollywood was having a field day knitting scarlet letters. But all that has changed, too. Goldie and Bill got married, and they are now the happy old-fashioned parents of a son named Oliver, born in September, 1976. "Show business with its transitory and superficial values is not the most important thing in my life," said Goldie at the time, and proved it by dropping out for two years.

"I ended up paying my husband seventy-five thousand dollars to get out of that marriage, and I went through some rough times, but everything is terrific now. I am deliriously happy. And I've decided to work again," she says. She just completed a new film with Chevy Chase called *Foul Play*, and by the time you read this, she'll be in Rome co-starring in a new Italian film with Giancarlo Giannini. But movies are not her prime interest, a fact she demonstrates by continually interrupting any discussion of her life as a movie star to chase the baby around the room, change his diapers, feed him an exotic sip of white wine, and perform a juggling act with five bread rolls he is trying to stuff into his mouth simultaneously.

"I really shouldn't do interviews," she sighs, momentarily calming down the noise with a brand-new bottle for Baby. "I mean, people will really think I sound so boring. But the truth is that I have always wanted a family and now that I'm a mother, Bill and I take our family life very seriously. We both come from very close families." Instead of showing off the 8 x 10 glossies from her latest movie, Goldie gets out the Polaroids of her family Christmas reunion in the new house she's designed and built—"a Grant Wood American Gothic Victorian gingerbread beach house with a red tile roof on a cliff overlooking the Pacific Ocean." She's as homespun and wholesome as a Girl Scout cookie.

The new California beach house is a spitball's throw from Katharine Ross, Billy Wilder and Dyan Cannon, but Goldie doesn't know any of them. "It's like we're in the woodwork and we come out to do our shopping. We never go to parties. I don't get invited to them, really, because I never went and they all just stopped asking me. I went to Sue Mengers' house once and I was very uncomfortable. People were all very stilted and self-conscious and everybody just stared at each other. It had nothing to do with Sue Mengers. She was funny, smart and a great hostess. But I'm doing business on the phone all day long so I don't want to go out at night and listen to the same people I've been doing business with on the phone, all doing business over dinner. I couldn't wait to get home, put on my pajamas, make myself a cup of tea, listen to my music, and not talk at all. There are so many more fulfilling things to do than going to parties. Motherhood is so demanding that I don't have much energy left over at the end of the day for parties."

When she works, she drags the baby along, too. "Wherever I am in the world, I kiss Oliver good-bye in the morning and I am always there to put him to bed at night. He's a very solid citizen. I will not have a neurotic Hollywood child on my hands. I am truly blessed because Bill wants the same things I do. If I'm sleepy in the morning, he gets up, gives Oliver his bottle, changes his diaper, and gets back into bed before I wake up. There is absolutely no comparison between this marriage and my first marriage. I was so young and idealistic and there just wasn't anything meaningful about that marriage. It only lasted three years. Then it took another three years to get out of it. My family was always very close and that's what I wanted. I started making movies just to have something to do because I wasn't happy at home. My mother and father are separated and they still live in the same house. And it might seem like an old-fashioned concept, but I think the family unit is something you can depend on even if everything else fails. Now that I have a secure homelife that I don't have to work for, I'm having more fun with my career and I think it has made me a much more accomplished actress. I had enough of those years of working just to pay my bills. Now I intend to work whenever I feel like it just to please myself."

She's paid her dues. She grew up in Takoma Park, Maryland, a very average student with no aspirations. All she wanted to do was dance. Her father was a violinist, her mother ran a dancing school. Goldie taught dancing for a while after high school, then went to Williamsburg and acted in passion plays in a three-thousand-seat amphitheater. Then she got a job in the World's Fair and moved to New York. She lived in a building on Eighth Avenue "that is now overrun with prostitutes" and got turned down as a Copa girl. To pay the rent, she worked as a go-go dancer in a strip joint in New Jersey. "I made twenty dollars a night for dancing my buns off and this sleazy agent got five dollars of that. I used to dance in sequin pasties on tabletops with guys exposing themselves and I ended up hitching a ride back to New York on a Mack truck. I really don't believe the things I went through, but I wanted to be in show business so desperately. I went to Puerto Rico and worked with a rock band and spent my last two hundred dollars on a dog because I was so lonely. I was ready to throw in the towel when a choreographer friend called and asked me to go to California. I left my four roommates, my furniture and my boyfriend, packed my dog, went to Hollywood, and never came back."

Things didn't happen overnight there, either. "I got a little apartment across the street from Disneyland and ended up in a chorus line in Las Vegas. I was up all night, sleeping all day, and I turned into a zombie. I saw myself one day on TV in a red wig, looking like somebody's pet monkey. That's when I quit. It was a crappy life. I went back to L.A., gave myself two weeks and if I didn't make it, I promised my parents I'd come home to Maryland." One day before the deadline, she landed a bit part in an Andy Griffith TV special. An agent from William Morris spotted her, got her three segments on "Laugh-In," and that was the beginning of Goldie Hawn. Billy Wilder saw the show one night, called Mike Frankovich, the producer, and he put her in *Cactus Flower*. A star was born and an Oscar was won. "My greatest regret is that I won the Oscar before I learned how to act. I'd love another crack at it now. I've learned so much about acting and life and everything."

Self-assured after taking time off to rethink her priorities, Goldie is running her life now. Her head is glued on under that mop of hairdresser's joy with all the right tacks. "I met my first husband when I was a chorus girl. I was so green, such a baby. He was a father figure to me. Then I met Bill on an airplane. We have the same sense of humor, the same needs, similar family backgrounds. I always felt temporary when I was married before. Now I feel mature enough to know what love is. It's a big responsibility. People are so easy, money is so easy, there are so many divorces in Hollywood. Yesterday I sat down and tried to figure out who my real friends are. Except for Lee Grant, I don't have any actress friends. My best friend owns a carpet mill. And that's a wonderful feeling, not to owe anybody anything. When I told my mother I was pregnant she said, 'Don't tell anybody! Get your divorce right away! You'll ruin your career!' But times have changed. Nobody did one thing to me. I've had no repercussions, no DAR ladies picketing the Academy Awards. I'm living my own life. And I have more courage now to take chances with my career."

In *Foul Play* she plays a mousy librarian who gets chased by a scar-faced strangler, an albino killer, a black limousine with a Turkish chauffeur and an evil dwarf because a hitchhiker has deposited in her cigarettes some secret microfilm containing plans to assassinate the Pope. "It's silly, it's crazy!" She laughs hysterically. "But a lot of it is scary, too. At one point I almost get stabbed with knitting needles. We got the guy who owns Magnin's in San Francisco to play the Pope. I think he's Jewish. And I did all of my own stunt work.

There is one shot that will take you right out of the seat. I think it's better than *Bullitt*. I had to drive seventy miles an hour down those steep hills and I'm terrified of cars. I don't know why I did it. It must have been the money. I did hairpin turns, spun out of control, and got chased fifty-five feet up in the air on suspended catwalks over the city. I was up there two days and finally got vertigo and they had to throw me against the wall to keep me from falling through the ceiling of the Shrine auditorium."

Goldie has pruned away the clutter in her private life to make room for a career when the right parts come along and now she can go away without worries. She isn't rich, although she's made some money in real estate. Her overhead has been reduced. She does most of her own housework and keeps a nanny for Oliver. She's trying to talk her mother into moving to California permanently. "I still get a lot of pleasure out of acting, but now I've reached the level where I can say, 'Hey, it was great working with you and I'll see you around.' I don't feel I've got to call up actors and say, 'Let's get together and keep this thing going.' I go home at night to the real world now. I've changed. I'm more solid inside myself as a person. The rest is just cake." There's still some Goldie in those Hollywood hills.

11

NATALIE & R. J. WAGNER

BEVERLY HILLS, CALIFORNIA. THEY WERE HOT. THEN THEY WERE cold. Now they've gone on to another plateau. In Hollywood, where yesterday's movie-company executives are today's mechanics, Natalie Wood and Robert Wagner are not only survivors, they're durables. They've done a terrific job of growing up in an insane business that treated them as teen-age commodities, and now they are real people who still maintain tremendously respected professional statuses. The Wagners have played the game and won.

For further proof, examine *Cat on a Hot Tin Roof* on NBC-TV December 6. Natalie—full-bodied, womanly, dizzyingly gorgeous—is Tennessee Williams' famous Maggie the Cat. R.J. (nobody who knows him personally ever calls him anything but R.J.) plays Brick with an astonishing depth and sensitivity that is going to knock viewers on their skeptical ears. Laurence Olivier is Big Daddy. Maureen Stapleton is Big Mama and the director is Robert (*Murder by Death*) Moore. Mark down the date. December 6. It's become an important date in the Wagner household. December 6 is the date, years ago, when they proudly admit with only a slight blush that "we first met—intimately."

It's a night for such revelations. Their lifelong cook, bottle washer and household organizer, "the great Willie Mae," has shaken up the house by taking a night off. R.J. has cooked spaghetti, old friend and Natalie's ex-secretary Mart (*The Boys in the Band*) Crowley has made the salad, everyone has made a brief but insincere stab at washing the dishes, six-year-old Natasha has done a provocative tango to extend her bedtime curfew, and there's some fancy dog-barking and baby-screaming from two-year-old Courtney in the bedroom above. In the middle of the chaos the Wagners are trying to give an interview in the luxurious den of their magnificent Cape Cod farmhouse, once owned by Patti Page, in the heart of the plastic paradise called Beverly Hills.

In a long, rambling conversation that extended into the predawn hours, the first subject on their minds was, of course, the TV special, which came about because Laurence Olivier has always loved Natalie's work.

"We first met him through Spencer Tracy." She nods sleepily, sipping the residue of a deep Burgundy that matches her eyes. "He was fond of R.J. and wanted us to meet Olivier. Then, through the years, we've seen a lot of him."

When he's in Los Angeles, he swims in their pool and has vacationed on their yacht. Three times he's asked Natalie to appear with him in films. It was only natural that when he made his TV deal for British tributes to the American theater, he'd choose *Cat* for his first production, with the Wagners in mind. "It was a lucky break for us. Everyone adjusted schedules so R.J. could do it during his break from the 'Switch' series. We rehearsed for four weeks in London, blocked it just like a play, and by the time we got to Manchester, we could have gone onstage and played it. The whole thing was taped in nine days."

Olivier rebuilt the dressing rooms with closed-circuit TV so the Wagners could watch each other when they weren't onstage together and baby-sit at the same time. "The accent wasn't a problem, because we've both played Southerners before," says R.J. "It was a question of balance. Working together is easier if you're married—you can cue each other in bed, in the shower, over the breakfast table. What's hard is turning it off after a dramatic scene so you don't take Maggie and Brick home at night."

Natalie started smoking profusely again in the part, a habit she's still trying to lick. R.J. found it a "big downer" to work with both a crutch and a drink in every scene. "You can get self-pitying in that trap, then you lose the audience." Both of them have only adoration for Olivier, who intimidates most screen actors. "He chose not to do any suggestion of Burl Ives. He didn't play up the physical bigness of Big Daddy. His power as an actor does all of that. He took his direction just like everyone else and never interfered with Bob Moore's staging. It was probably the best working experience we've ever had."

The world thinks of them as a team, but they've only worked together twice—in an MGM bomb called *All the Fine Young Cannibals* and a TV movie called "The Affair." "They confuse us with our marriages," giggles Natalie. They were Hollywood's dream couple. Then they divorced, married other people, and life's circuitous route led back to their front doors again. Over the years, they ran into each other bashfully at parties, but remained remote. At the same time, they had remained close to each other's family, so there were some ties they never severed—"including the emotional ties between us," says Natalie. "We should never have broken up in the first place."

R.J. read about her divorce from Richard Gregson, called up to offer his sympathy, and they started discussing their personal difficulties like mature friends. Then, on January 26, 1972, he invited her for a weekend in Palm Springs. Was it a nervous weekend? "It was . . ." she gropes for the right word, then collapses in a tumble of laughs, "completely mind-blowing!"

They lived so quietly in Palm Springs that nobody knew, including their best friends. No paparazzi, no nosy neighbors. Then they remarried on July 16, 1972, and moved to Natalie's house in Brentwood, then R.J.'s house in Palm Springs, a Malibu beach house, a lake house in Tahoe. It was almost as though they were trying out the new marriage on different movie sets. "Now," R.J. says firmly, "for the first time we have everything out of storage, under one roof, in only one house with one husband, one wife and one family."

"There was never any problem with what to give us for wedding presents," says Natalie, "just bring back the old furniture! We still had all of our old monogrammed sheets, towels and stationery."

How is this marriage different from the first one? "We have the same pressures as before, but more responsibilities, too. Besides Natasha and Courtney, who are with us all the time, there's Katie, R.J.'s daughter, who is twelve. Then we're close to R.J.'s ex-stepsons Josh and Peter, and Richard Gregson's three children by a marriage prior to Natalie, who live in London.

"Luckily, all of the kids, dogs and cats get along. But we have more personal ties, a bigger house to run. Also, the industry has changed, too. We have fewer superficial demands made on our time than when we were young contract players."

Natalie is a superb mother. She'd probably turn down an Oscar (she's been nominated three times) if it coincided inconveniently with one of her children's birthdays. "I thought it would be so easy to have babies," she says, wide-eyed. "But it demands concentration. I had no problem with Natasha, but with Courtney, it was a disaster. I was fully awake and watched the whole thing in a mirror until they ran into difficulties and had to perform an emergency Caesarean. The umbilical cord was wrapped around her neck three times and a whole team of doctors were running around in white coats yelling 'Emergency section—emergency pediatric intensive care—get up here on the double!' The last thing I remember them doing is throwing a white sheet over the mirror so I couldn't see the knife. I kept yelling, 'Cut! I want a retake!' I felt like I was on the wrong set and the scene was from somebody else's picture!"

Except for a role in a never-released detective spoof with Michael Caine called *Peeper*, which she did while she was still breast-feeding Courtney, Natalie hasn't worked in films since the box-office bonanza *Bob & Carol & Ted & Alice* (1969). While R.J. toils on TV in one successful series after another, her career has taken a cheerful back seat. "I did all the fighting, the eighteen-month suspensions, the whole bit. There comes a time when you have to recharge your batteries. I've worked steadily and consistently since I was five years old and there were serious gaps in those years when I should've been learning about how to live. I think if your whole impetus and all of your priorities come from your career, there's something missing in a person.

"My first child was born in 1970, and I was already past thirty. I just wanted to take care of a family for a change. In Hollywood, what they don't understand is that working can be a choice. Then when you do find something you really want to do, it's the hardest thing in the world to get off the ground.

"Careers are strange things. You can't plan them and you can't second-guess them. You've got to go on instinct. That's the only way I've ever been able to do it. How the hell can you be objective about your own work?"

"You never know when you're going to be hot or cold," says R.J. "I've been doing it for twenty-five years and I'm still working, so I consider myself a success. But I've had a lot of body blows. In order to keep working, I've had to do the TV series. But they're nothing to be snobbish about. They're damned hard to do. I work ten hours a day, nine months a year, so I can afford to do something meaningful like *Cat on a Hot Tin Roof*."

"I'm luckier," Natalie interrupts. "I don't have to work just to keep a career going. My emotional stability doesn't depend on whether I'm acting or not. Those days of doing movies I hate just to make money are over for me. You slave over something you really care about—in my case, it was *Inside Daisy Clover*—and it flops.

"Then when you make your biggest hit—the one where you make the most money—it's not the one you want to be remembered for. Mine was *Bob and Carol and Ted and Alice*, which made me a personal fortune. I enjoyed making it, but it wasn't anything I desperately, passionately cared about. It's a crap shoot."

In movies like *Splendor in the Grass* and *Inside Daisy Clover*, Natalie reached tumultuous emotional highs, but R.J. has a lot of talent that hasn't been utilized on film until *Cat*. "Well," he says, "I haven't read a script in a long time that had that kind of part for a man. Look at the ones that do get made. It took them ten years to get *Cuckoo's Nest* off the ground."

"Even for women, the parts are scarce," adds Natalie. "I've only read one script lately that made me say, 'Oh, wow! What a part!' and I couldn't play it. She was *black*!"

When the laughter subsides, the joke is on Hollywood. In a town where being a movie star and happy at the same time makes you an immediate suspect, the Wagners don't care what anyone thinks. Their critics come and go through revolving doors, but like the love in the song by Gershwin, they're here to stay.

12

NATALIE WOOD

HOLLYWOOD. THERE'S A NEW SAYING IN HOLLYWOOD: THE MORE IT costs, the less fun it is to make. The two hundred actors, technicians and stunt men waiting to be drowned in mud on MGM's Stage 30 are finding this out.

For three months they've been fighting horrors from outer space on a $16-million extravaganza called *Meteor*. Bags of white powdered cement are being sifted into Karl Malden's hair. Sean Connery, moustached and dapper, is covered with dirt. Natalie Wood has narrowly escaped being crushed by a falling chandelier. Now they are waiting for the mud.

Stage 30 is the old Esther Williams swimming pool, where fishy aquamusicals were made in MGM's youth. Instead of Esther, feather-stroking her way into a close-up to Cole Porter music like a smiling porpoise, the tank today contains one million pounds or eight thousand dollars' worth of warm, slimy bentonite—a wet clay ooze used by oil-field drillers—that forms part of the already-estimated eight million dollars used for special effects on the picture.

"We've done all the straightforward stuff," groans Natalie Wood. "Now we're ready for the blood and guts, where everyone ends up wounded or dead."

Some of the other "stuff" includes a scene in which New York City gets buried under tons of rock, Hong Kong gets washed into the sea, and an avalanche in the Austrian Alps collapses a mountain village under 300 million tons of snow.

On Stage 30, which American International Pictures is renting from MGM to film *Meteor*, the New York subway system will be drowned in mud heated to 70 degrees. Underground pumps will drive it back into the trapped cars where hundreds of extras dressed like commuters will scream their heads off in the rush-hour panic. Token booths, turnstiles, escalators, express stops, tile walls, even the graffiti will get blown to smithereens.

The actors are understandably nervous. "The problem," says Sean Connery, "is not how to act, but how to survive." Ronald Neame, the director, has a bigger worry. "These sets cost millions of dollars, and once we blow up the pipes and the mud collapses, we've got to do it in one take or we cannot go back and do it over again."

Back on Stage 27, where the Emerald City was located for *The Wizard of Oz*, there is some last-minute work still undone on the space center, where the meteor hits Manhattan. There is shattered glass everywhere, busted TV screens, and a man is spraying smoke on the actors from a milk container. The big meteor, five miles wide, has hit the space center, located beneath the subway system.

Malden is the head of NASA. Connery is an astrophysicist from MIT. Brian Keith is his Russian counterpart. Natalie Wood is a Russian astrophysicist who acts as Keith's interpreter. She's the only actress in Hollywood who could play the role because she's bilingual.

"My tongue has new muscles," she jokes. "Brian Keith's Russian is written phonetically on the script pages in English, but I had to really speak in real Russian. I've been speaking Russian all of my life, but for this one I had to study two hours a day for two months so I could say things like 'If Peter the Great doesn't exist, we're in big trouble.' My dialogue is written in the Cyrillic alphabet. By the time I was ten, I could speak Russian fluently, and I still have never been to Russia. But I knew I was good when I started arguing with the teacher. One day the teacher was gone, and I had to say 'Ignition accomplished, progress normal.' I was stuck. So I called my father in Palm Springs and asked him how to say it and he said, 'They didn't say things like that when I was in Russia.' I spouted a lot of Russian gibberish. Nobody knew the difference."

Sean Connery, who hasn't worked in Hollywood since *The Molly Maguires* ten years ago, lives in Spain for tax purposes. "I spent forty weeks a year away from home when I lived in England and spent ninety-eight percent of my income in taxes. I had to get out. Now I'm learning to like Los Angeles again. I have more energy here. I get up at six A.M., drink half a gallon of milk, and I'm on my way. Then when I get to the studio, they cover me with a ton of stuff that stays wet, slimy and colder than hell. It looks like chocolate pudding, but it tastes like @*#!"

Ronald Neame goes about his business amidst the chaos of exploding walls and falling beams with the calm reserve of a British stockbroker. Having already directed *The Poseidon Adventure*, he knows the ins and outs of disaster epics like the markings on a rural map. "Up until *Poseidon,* I was a boy who did art-house pictures like *The Prime of Miss Jean Brodie.* Now I get nothing but disaster blockbusters. I turn most of them down, but I chose to do this one because it says more than most.

"Here's this meteor, five miles wide, flying at the earth going thirty thousand miles an hour, and a chunk of it hits the AT and T Building and drives the populace under the Hudson River, and if the rest of it hits the earth, the impact would be ten times the greatest earthquake ever recorded. They've got six days to divert it from its course.

"The Americans are forced to admit they've got a satellite orbiting the earth with nuclear warheads aimed at Russia. President Henry Fonda makes a speech to the world asking the Russians to join in, and the United Nations pressures the Russians into admitting they've got the same kind of satellite. So both sides have got to work out a plan to divert the meteor. Natalie Wood is the link between the two nations. It was the only legitimate way to have a girl in the picture."

Neame says the problem with this kind of picture is that "the minute I manage to solve one problem, there's another one. Yesterday we had a massive explosion and nobody was hurt. So when I finish demolishing the space center, I'll go home Friday night and start working on the mud. I'm in a perpetual state of anxiety. I get through each day at a time. Yesterday the roof collapsed and we spent

$150,000 on that trick for eleven seconds of screen time. I don't want to spend my life directing great big buggers like this, but it's easier to find sixteen million dollars than it is to find two. A movie's got to be bloodthirsty and brutal, or sexy or provocative, or contain some kind of shock value to get an audience.

"I was saluted by critics for *Jean Brodie,* assaulted for *Poseidon Adventure*, so what can I do? I've never been a rich man, so I did *Poseidon* because I had five percent of the picture. Then I waited a long time, saying no to junk films, trying to get some lovely scripts made. I couldn't get them financed. But I'd go round the bend if I wasn't doing something! So here I am, doing another disaster flick.

"This movie has already been sold to television and another studio bought it for overseas. Run Run Shaw put up money for distribution in Hong Kong. The Japanese put up money for Japan. They'll all presell it to theaters before it's even completed. They'll make back their investment before the movie is even seen. So we are talking about money, and that's why movies like *Meteor* are being made and others are not."

Natalie Wood, who has been a fixture in the motion-picture industry since the days of diapers and lollipops, is even more rueful. "When I was eight years old, I made a picture at Fox called *Miracle on Thirty-fourth Street*. It was made in black and white, nobody at the studio cared about it, all the publicity money went to *Forever Amber* and big Tyrone Power costume epics, which failed abominably at the box office, while our little film made tons of money and became a Christmas classic.

"It's always been like that in Hollywood. The whole thing is a comment on the decline of the movie industry. Here on the MGM lot, they've still got the dressing rooms where Greta Garbo had her permanent apartment. It's all gray and empty and covered with dust. I never go in there except to shampoo my hair."

At $16 million, *Meteor* will have to make $60 million just to break even. Neame says the financiers aren't worried. "The hardware will get them in. It's an entertainment. I do this stuff reasonably well because I was a cameraman. I did the early war films, I know the cutting room, I know how to use quick cuts to create excitement. But give me Maggie Smith anytime. After this one, I will never do anything again for money. With the right script, I will work for nothing.

That's a solemn promise. The next one will be something meaningful to me.

"This one won't be rubbish," he says, looking around to see if the bosses are listening, "but it won't be *The Prime of Miss Jean Brodie*, either."

13

LIZA MINNELLI

It's high noon in the Monday traffic of midtown Manhattan and on the seventh floor of a seedy building on Seventh Avenue, Liza Minnelli is lying on the floor of a recording studio listening to a playback. It's the day they are finally getting around to recording the original cast album of her Broadway musical *The Act*, and Liza is understandably nervous.

The place is crawling with union reps, lawyers, technicians, musicians and chorus girls, who started piling in at eleven thirty. The star was there two hours earlier, accompanied by her dog Hedy, a half-dachshund, half-cocker spaniel named after Hedy Lamarr. After the usual round of shoplifting jokes to break the ice, Liza tied Hedy to a chair with a piece of string, passed out a box of chocolates to the chorus kids, and started to work. Through the glass wall of the control room, she watched intensely as Stanley Lebowsky, the conductor of *The Act*, communicated with the backup singers, who were nervously twitching in a sealed glass recording booth with earphones on their heads. "Girls, when you come in on the words 'Movies rated X,' make it breathier and dirtier!" Everyone was working hard and fast to finish the orchestral passages by five o'clock and avoid paying overtime. "Cut down the air conditioning in the isolation booth, please," said Mr. Lebowsky over the loudspeaker system that was piped into the control room. "If it gets too cold in there, the kids will have pitch problems!"

Above the isolation booth, a movie screen hung precariously. Two days earlier, Diana Ross was watching the rushes from *The Wiz* on that screen while recording her voice on the sound track. Propped against the wall were the leftover sets from a Paul Simon road tour. The mikes Liza would be using had already been used by Judy Collins, Phoebe Snow, Quincy Jones, John Travolta and dozens of rock groups. "It looks like a scene from *Inside Daisy Clover*," she joked, easing the tension. "Remember the scene where Natalie Wood went bananas in the recording session? I will try not to go bananas."

Despite the gossip-column reports of nerves, fatigue and illness, Liza seemed fit as a fiddle. Her voice was hoarse and she chain-smoked Marlboros. Every so often she would let out a roaring whoop, the kind of yell cowboys make at rodeos. "It relaxes my throat muscles," she explained. But when she tried her first solo with the band, she quipped, "The Schuberts present B. S. Pully in *The Act*!" and there was a half-serious undertone in the laugh.

There is understandable anxiety at every recording session, but a special climate of adrenaline spiraled thicker than cigar smoke through the sessions for *The Act*. Most people think all you have to do to make an original cast album of a Broadway show is put a star (in this case, Liza) in front of a microphone. In truth, the legal clearances, red tape and labyrinthian chaos surrounding such a venture is tantamount to a rocket launching. In the case of *The Act*, there's even more complexity than usual. The fact that it will finally see its way to vinyl at all is a tribute to perseverance. "It was a case of crossed signals," says Liza to everyone who asks why the Broadway cast album has been so long in the making. "Columbia Records had an agreement to do the album, but the show's producers weren't interested, so nobody nudged them. Then while we were on the road my contract with Columbia expired. Also, they lost interest in show albums and started making rock albums that would sell faster. Then the show opened and nobody knew how to classify it. Was it a one-woman show or a Broadway musical? Then we couldn't get the record out for the Christmas market. Then everybody thought everybody else was working on it. People were asking for the album in the lobby, strangers were calling up asking when it was coming out, and we didn't know what to tell them. We had a hit show, sold out every night, and nobody wanted to record it. It was embarrassing."

Fred Ebb and John Kander, Liza's longtime friends and composers of the score, were baffled. "It's still a mystery. We've had flop shows that were recorded the week they opened. But nobody seemed interested in this one."

At this point, a man named Hugh Fordin entered the picture. Fordin had written books on Arthur Freed's days at MGM and Oscar Hammerstein. He owned a record company called DRG Records, and had previously released a series of highly successful outtakes cut from movie musicals as well as the cast album for *Very Good Eddie*. Fordin called Kander and Ebb with an invitation to record some of their songs that had been deleted from old shows in out-of-town tryouts for nostalgia buffs. They said, "Well, if you want our songs, how about recording *The Act*?" Everyone agreed, but the financial imbroglio was just beginning. Liza waived her salary, but author George Furth had to be paid, even though none of his words are spoken on the record. The show's press agent, company manager, even the four actors who do not sing in the show had to be paid union minimum. The seven chorus kids wanted a share of the profits in addition to a week's salary, but finally agreed to waive their contractual rights just to get the record out. Even former chorus kids who are no longer in the show but appear in taped portions of songs heard in the theater get paid. Even after cutting costs to the bone, what started out as a relatively simple record will end up costing in excess of $50,000. It ain't easy bein' green.

Obstacles surmounted, the recording day arrived and forty weeks and more than three hundred performances after *The Act* first opened, it was finally heading for the phonograph. "The Musicians Union says the orchestra can only record fifteen minutes of actual music per three-hour session," groaned Hugh Fordin. It was costing him two hundred dollars an hour for studio rental, not counting the recording equipment, synthesizers, etc. In the control room, about a million buttons were being punched by a recording engineer while thirty lighted panels recorded sound waves and noise levels. A watchdog from the Musicians Union who looked like Basil Rathbone watched the clock and stopped the music as soon as the time was up.

"Ready for the verse to 'City Lights,' Liza!"

"Wouldn't it be swell if something great came out, like a voice?" She smiled at the drummer, who played for Judy Garland at Carnegie Hall, and took her place in the isolation booth. She popped her first *p* on the word "porch" so loud that Stanley Lebowsky's earphones blew out. On the first perfect take, a teen-age fan opened the door to the studio and it all had to be done over again. "I've been here since eleven this morning," said the guilty culprit, ponytail bobbing. "I cut school today and everything. I've seen *The Act* eight times!"

"We ain't got enough problems, now we got the Liza freaks climbing in through the windows," moaned an engineer.

Through it all, Liza was in high spirits, Fred Ebb only a step away from her elbow, even inside the soundproof isolation booth. (If you hear any strange noises on the record when it comes out, they'll be Fred Ebb's nerves frying.) But Ebb and Kander are not only the composers, they're Liza's big brothers. After each take, she looks to them for approval. "Liza, sing the verse a bit softer, honey," says Kander, and the star obliges.

Liza's got earphones on her head, a lighted Marlboro in one hand, and the other hand is clenched into a fist while she sings "My secret isn't diet, drugs or pills—I've simply found a new routine to banish all my ills!" The words come out, strong and full of passion, and even the surliest heart will have to make emotional connections between the singer and the song. By the time she got to the big "Shine It On" number, her voice had gone from a bass fiddle to a brassy trumpet. "All I needed was warming up." She beamed, feeling good. The juices were flowing now, but the earphones kept short-circuiting, leaving the musicians deaf and causing endless delays. Hugh Fordin managed miraculously to hide his mounting hysteria as the overtime mounted.

A thousand dollars after 5 P.M., the orchestra finished playing, the musicians went home, and Liza was left alone on the set like an orphan in the storm, singing with a solo mike while the prerecorded instrumental sections played through her headset. "My level's fine—could you bring up the violins?" she asked. She blows the lyrics. The engineer blows the transmitter. During the breaks, Liza improvises "South America Take It Away" and listens to playbacks like an expectant parent outside a delivery room.

The tongue-twisting lyrics keep tripping over her tongue, even though she's sung them thousands of times. Freb Ebb sits on a folding chair in front of her mike, mouthing the words while she sings. Whenever he frowns, she stops, says "What now?" and takes criticism like a star pupil. During ten straight hours of toil, the only thing she asked for was a higher stool to sit on. Even in her exhaustion, there is no display of temperament or impatience. "Could I just hear the first eight bars again?" she asks. Then, "Is that OK with everybody?"

By 9 P.M., they've got an album in the can and for the first time that day, Liza loosens her muscles and collapses on the sofa in a puddle of grins. "I am dead," she sighs, "but I gotta admit this was a swell bunch of people to sing for."

The original Broadway cast album of *The Act* will be out in two weeks. We'll see what happens.

Dorothy McGuire JOHN SWOPE

Goldie Hawn

TERRY O'NEILL

Natalie Wood and R. J. Wagner with daughters Courtney and Natasha

Natalie Wood PHOTO © MICHAEL CHILDERS/SYGMA

Roger Moore and his family

PHOTO © PHILIPPE LEDRU/SYGMA

Liza Minnelli PHOTO © DIRCK HALSTEAD/SYGMA

Melina Mecouri

FROM THE AUTHOR'S COLLECTION

Marsha Mason

14

ROGER MOORE

When the late Ian Fleming sold the rights to twelve James Bond novels to producers Harry Saltzman and Albert Broccoli in 1960, he did it to set up a trust fund for his children. He hated movies, saw only two in his life (*Gone with the Wind* and *Cavalcade*), and hated the choice of Sean Connery as 007. He died four years later, still hating the James Bond movies, but Broccoli is still turning them out and will keep turning them out until he runs out of hardware.

Nobody can tell one James Bond movie from another anymore, but nobody cares. They make 'em big and they make 'em expensive and there's a brainless audience out there in the unwashed swamp of indiscriminate moviegoers that eats 'em up as fast as they can make 'em.

Ian Fleming didn't care for Sean Connery, who got rich on the Bond movies and then got sick of them. He wouldn't have approved of George Lazenby, who made one Bond film and then retired from show business to go off to a monastery to meditate. And the man who gave birth to James Bond in print, describing him as a skinny man with a scar on his face (his ideal choice for the role was always

Hoagy Carmichael), would be hard put for an explanation of Roger Moore.

"I don't know why they picked me," says Moore, grinning, a forty-nine-year-old actor who has often been described as prettier than his leading ladies, "but the money is fantastic."

It sure is. Moore originally signed for three Bond films and now he's talking about renewing for a fourth. He gets a staggering salary plus a hefty percentage of each film's gross, and all of the Bonds have made astoundingly healthy profits. Moore has become world-famous and filthy rich playing 007.

Yet in private life he's as much like James Bond as Tatum O'Neal. A soft-spoken gent with a beauty mark Elizabeth Taylor might envy, he seems more at home in an oatmeal cardigan from the Burlington Arcade, playing backgammon on a yacht in the South of France, than a daredevil secret agent in a rubber fin battling crocodiles, serpents, sexy villains and exploding submarines. "When I started out as an actor," he says wryly, "I thought I'd wear blazers and answer telephones. I'm still waiting."

In the tenth and latest James Bond epic, *The Spy Who Loved Me*, which hits the nation's screens this week, Roger Moore is facing new perils.

"It's twice the budget and twice the size on the screen. Most of the Bond pictures cost around seven million dollars. This one cost thirteen and a half million. We go back to the underwater bit. A car turns into a submarine that shoots ballistic missiles that knock out helicopters. There's a basic plot: The Russians and the British have lost Polaris submarines that get swallowed up in the bowels of a giant tanker owned by an evil villain named Fishfinger, who plans to blow up New York and Moscow. He has webbed fingers and lives underwater off the coast of Sardinia in a magnificent underwater city designed by Ken Adam, who did the sets for *Sleuth*. Every time he presses a button, all the pictures go up behind a sixty-foot dining table and reveal the ocean beyond filled with man-eating sharks. Just like a Beverly Hills screening room."

When Roger Moore talks about the Bond films, which he's paid handsomely to do, it's with the obvious tongue-in-cheek detachment of a wise fool who knows exactly which side of the toast has the butter. Getting the publicity out of the way as fast as possible, he continues: "The sets are so enormous they had to build new sound stages at Pinewood, fill them with water, then blow them up. They set up eight cameras to get the explosions, then dropped sixty-five billion gallons of water on us when they torpedoed the underwater city, and it washed the director, Lew Gilbert, right out of the tank. We had to shoot the whole thing over again, which didn't go over very well because it came right after the drought in England."

Does he ever get injured? "Constantly. I am convinced the producers are trying to kill me for the insurance. I now have four holes in my backside from a chair that blew up before I could get out of it. I've had concussions, bruises and scars all over my body from these films. I cracked my kneecap, dislocated my shoulder and smashed up a speedboat going fifty miles per hour and knocked out all of my teeth. Listen, it is obvious I don't do this for my health. I do it for money. All I really want to do is wear blazers and answer telephones."

Moore says he's done the Bond character so much the only things he looks forward to on each new Bond film are "the stunts and special effects. The fun of it now is sitting around on the set trying to think up new gag lines.

"Some of the best James Bond lines in the Sean Connery versions were ad libs he made up on camera. They cut my best ad lib in this new one. I fired a gun right at Curt Jurgens' groin and said 'Ball's-eye, Fishfinger!' and they thought it was too outrageous. But I did talk them into leaving one thing in—at one point, a submarine turns into a sports car, rides up on the beach, the occupants roll down the window and throw a fish out." These are the jokes, folks.

Has he ever thought about diversifying the image? "Every waking moment. But the men who put up the money for movies today want at least twenty-five explosions and a speedboat flying through the air when they think of me, and if a script doesn't have those elements, then they say, 'Oh, then let's go for Robert Redford.'

"I'm dying to do a romantic comedy, but the problem is there aren't any romantic comedies around for men. When I was managing director of Brut Productions, the film division of Fabergé, I was responsible for finding and getting them to make *A Touch of Class*. My only mistake was not casting myself in it. But I don't think the Bond pictures have hindered my career. I think they're just another extension of my tiny talent."

His capacity for self-parody is disarming. One gets the impression that he doesn't take his career any more seriously than the critics do. Yet there's an underlying need to reestablish firmer roots in acting out roles of more substance, and it comes to the surface like cream rising to the top of lukewarm coffee when the Bond press-agentry is over and done with and Moore is able to relax and be himself. "I've been terribly lucky because I went from the 'Maverick' TV series to the 'Saint' TV series to James Bond and been typed in every one of them and still I've never been out of work. If anything, I've managed to confuse everyone."

The son of a London policeman, Moore started out as a cartoonist and tea server in a publicity office. An extra job in a Shakespearean movie led to drama classes, modeling, and eventually a trip to America, where he ended up at the tail end of the old MGM era, toiling in a costume epic called *Diane*. It still turns up on the late show to haunt him. "It had some of the most terrible dialogue ever written, despite the fact that it was a Christopher Isherwood screenplay. Every time I see it, I crack up at one line I say to Lana Turner.

"I played a rough-and-tumble prince who only wants to wrestle and hunt stags. So she's brought in by my father, who says, 'Turn him into a real prince.' So Lana takes this raw youth and obeys the instructions of the court, and I turn to her and say, 'You made me a prince—now make me a king!' I'd love to remake that turkey with Anita Bryant and say, 'Now make me a queen!' "

The films in his Hollywood period were all about like that. He lost Elizabeth Taylor to Van Johnson in *The Last Time I Saw Paris*, got upstaged by Ann Blyth's horse in *The King's Thief*, and in *The Miracle*, with Carroll Baker, he led a parade of soldiers through the streets of Brussels in Rosalind Russell's leftover costumes from *Auntie Mame*. He fled Hollywood in 1955, ended up in Yugoslav spaghetti spectaculars, met an Italian temptress named Luisa in something called *The Rape of the Sabine Women*, and they've been making their own spaghetti ever since. Mrs. James Bond, as she hates to be called, is happy with Roger's new fame but disgusted with the image.

Besides the "You are lovely—you are hideous—you remind me of my nephew" fans, he's developed a cult of unruly female camp followers. One girl last year arrived at their country house near London and started sleeping under a tree. Luisa ran out in the yard and evicted her from the property. Luisa is his soulmate, bodyguard, and the mother of his three children—Deborah, thirteen, Jeffrey, eleven, and Christian, four.

"They're all pros," Moore says. "Jeff played my son in a TV movie about Sherlock Holmes. Deborah worked with me in a TV episode of 'The Persuaders' with Tony Curtis that I directed. But Luisa is the director at home. We have an understanding that I have the last word." What's that? "Yes, dear."

Between Bond pictures, he's done other action-packed bombs like *Street People* with Stacy Keach and *Gold* with Susannah York, but the Bond films have furnished him with the luxury of travel (the new one was filmed in Sardinia, Egypt, Scotland, England, Switzerland, the Bahamas and the Arctic Circle) and the opportunity to work with snakes, sharks and other exotic dangers. Doubles? "If it's a question of falling down sixty-four stairs, I get a double. If it's sixty-three, I can cope. The love scenes, of course, they have to use a double because Luisa is standing around with a bloody great knife. 'Do it,' she says, '—but don't enjoy it!' "

And the end result is that nobody takes it seriously, not even his kids. "One day I took Jeffrey to a posh restaurant for a man-to-man lunch, and he said, 'Could you beat up anybody in here?' I looked around and the patrons all looked rather old, so I said yes and he said, 'But what if James Bond came in?' I said, 'But, son, I *am* James Bond!' and he said, 'No, I mean the real one—Sean Connery!' "

For a man self-described as a "devout coward," Roger Moore has learned to take it on the chin, on-screen and off. "To look brave without flinching," grins 007, "—*that's* acting!"

15

MELINA MERCOURI

ATHENS. MELINA MERCOURI IS IN JAIL. IT'S NOT WHAT YOU THINK. No, she's not a prisoner. Only the jail is real. Melina is making a movie here, directed by her husband, Jules Dassin, the first film they've made in Greece since the fall of the military dictatorship. And here's the irony: they're making it in the fortresslike Koridalos Prison, where the colonels who made their lives a living hell for eight years of exile are themselves behind bars. It's a final retribution, and the feeling is so eerie Melina is almost stoic with awe.

Melina is sitting on an iron cot in the concrete cell that once belonged to Patakos, the same colonel who took away her citizenship and forced from her those tearful words that have now become part of Greek history: "I am born Greek, I will die Greek. You were born a Fascist, you will die a Fascist!" Across the hall, a tiny ray of light emerges from the door of another cell, where the dreaded leader of the junta, Papadopoulos, was jailed. Melina cannot rest until she sees that one, too. A jailer with a ring of iron keys unlocks the door and she peers inside. It's just like the other cell. She smiles wryly. "It's like a third-class hotel room. Except for the bars on the windows. I don't think it's enough punishment for the colonels. I am very nervous here. For me, I could have been in one of these cells like a snap of the fingers."

Memories flood the prison. Koridalos is in the heart of Piraeus, where Melina ran for a seat in Parliament in the Greek elections. It is the same prison where she attended the trials of the colonels on a journalist's pass after returning to Greece when her citizenship was restored with honor two years ago. The colonels have been moved to another prison across the street. Now the wing of cells where Melina is filming is empty, but in the distance you can hear the wails and moans of women prisoners. Some of them are Americans, arrested for dope smuggling. Nobody visits them except a priest from the American Embassy. The woman who serves Melina coffee is a trusty, serving life imprisonment for bashing in her husband's head with a mortar and pestle until it was the size of a pin. She smiles warmly, then shuffles back down the empty corridor until her footsteps disappear inside the echoing halls of the prison.

Melina shudders. "Every day when I was in exile, I had the fear of going to prison. Then I learned from the others who stayed behind to be tortured that prison was a relief. It was the end of torture. The real terror was the military police. Now they are all out free. Only a few of the colonels, the leaders, remain behind bars. They have television. They will probably be paroled in a few months or a few years. And life goes on. It doesn't seem fair, somehow."

Melina shrugs, then returns to the first cell. It has a stand-up toilet, a sink on the wall, a shelf for a newspaper, and an iron cot covered with an army blanket. There is a small filing cabinet that holds a comb, a mirror and a Thermos for water. The only window is set in heavy steel casement, and the only color in the drab cell comes from religious pictures, crucifixes, icons and the Virgin Mary on the wall. "Once you're locked in, you either blaspheme—or you pray!" says Melina. Through the bars of the cell, one sees only grim buildings the color of dirt. And in the distance, a guard with a rifle in the tower. Beyond, the purple sweep of the Greek mountains. It looks a bit like the back lot of a Hollywood studio. "Let's lock the door and see if it opens again," says Melina, mischievously. An electrician closes the door. We are flooded with darkness. The Virgin Mary's eyes seem to light up in the gloom. Then the door is opened again and the light comes in. "Ah, you see—I would survive!" She seems relieved.

Ellen Burstyn pokes her head in the door. "It doesn't seem as bad as the cells we see in American jails, but once they lock the door shut, you could get claustrophobia real fast." Burstyn is Melina's co-star. When she arrived, she shocked the Greeks when her chauffeur pointed out the Parthenon and Ellen asked: "And where is the Acropolis?" It made the Greek newspapers. Now things are running smoothly. All is forgiven. The two co-stars get along like sisters. And if the rumors on the set come true, they could both get Oscar nominations for this one.

The movie is tentatively called *A Dream of Passion*. It's about a famous Greek actress who returns to her native country after reaching international stardom to play Medea on the stage. As a publicity stunt, she is persuaded to visit an American woman who has been imprisoned for murdering her two children, Medea-style, as a revenge against an unfaithful husband. The actress is at first compassionate, then she becomes obsessed by the other woman's personality, until the two personas intertwine with dramatic and tragic results. If it sounds like Ingmar Bergman's *Persona*, the resemblance is not entirely coincidental. Jules Dassin admires him greatly. "Bergman was born to make guys like me sorry we didn't take up plumbing," he says modestly. There's a small homage to Bergman in the film where footage from *Persona* is projected, and Dassin is even toying with dedicating the film to him. But admiration is where the imitation ends and reality begins. The film is entirely original, based on a real case in which a real American killed her children and was imprisoned in Koridalos in 1960. She was kept four years, then released. Now she lives in America, where she's remarried with two new children of her own. The names have been changed to protect her, but the prison matrons remember her fondly, and some of them even write to her. This is the part Ellen Burstyn is playing.

Melina insists she identifies more with the American prisoner than the Greek film star. "I understand how you can love something so completely that you kill for it. I loved Dassin and, even more, I have loved Greece more than my own life—with an idealism that has become pathological," she says. Ellen says she doesn't identify with any of that but does "identify with the pain of being betrayed." She was in India attending a film festival in New Delhi when Jules Dassin contacted her by telegram. Then he called her at her hotel in Paris and discussed the role. Then he sent the script to her home in New York. "I wanted to like the script because I was dying to go to Greece. Also, it's part of the new revolution that's going on in films. Here at last is a chance to make a movie about two women relating to each other. Melina is really the star. My role is small in comparison. I only have two weeks' work. But we should all be able to do big parts, small parts, not be locked into stardom. It's very limiting to do only big parts. I did a tiny part in *Harry and Tonto* with Art Carney after I was nominated for two Oscars. I don't give a hoot about billing, money, or percentages." She closed in Chekhov's *Three Sisters* in Brooklyn, flew the next day to Athens. The noise from the American Express tours was too much for her in her plush hotel on Constitution Square, so she moved to a bungalow at the beach, an hour from the city. After she finishes her big dramatic scenes, she travels to the Berlin Film Festival, where she'll be on the jury, then to the Moscow Film Festival, and then returns to the States to begin the movie version of her Broadway hit, *Same Time, Next Year*, with Alan Alda.

Melina has no travel plans, except to bring her wildly successful *Medea* to America for a limited run. "Listen to me," she says soberly. "My life is in Greece now. Dassin was offered half a million to do a Charles Bronson movie. I was offered more than that to do a revival of *Can-Can* in Hollywood. Why? In all my life, I have never done anything to prove my talent. For me, *Never on Sunday* was a contribution because it brought Greece.to the world. *Phaedra* was a small contribution. But what else? The world has not seen my *Medea*, which the critics said revolutionized the Greek theater. The world did not see my *Streetcar Named Desire*. Only in Greece do they know how to appreciate me. Jules is sixty-two. I am fifty-one. At fifty-one, I'm going to move to Hollywood? No, I *am* Greece. We have not much money, but I don't want cars and houses and jewels. If I come to America, they want me to sing and dance and give up politics. I can't give up politics. I fear something will happen and—poof! I will be away making a film and never see Greece again."

Dassin, who after twenty-something years with this Greek fury, has finally started taking Greek lessons just so he can understand what's going on in his own house, is returning to his old style of filmmaking on the cheap. He has no distributor yet, although the word is out that the film is a winner and he's already getting calls from film festivals.

"I didn't want to turn this film over to the executive auctioneers of Hollywood or the university-bred Scheherazades of Madison Avenue. Agents and lawyers are running the business now. My last American film was *Up Tight* in 1968. My last Hollywood film was *Night and the City* with Gene Tierney and Richard Widmark in 1949. All those years when I was blacklisted, I learned to make better films for less money in Europe. This one is being made with Melina's money, my money, and loans from two friends in France and Switzerland. I financed it in one night. The last film I wrote, about the Lockheed scandal, took me two weeks just to get Ryan O'Neal on the phone. It still has not been made. This one is strictly a family film. If the film makes money, our friends who are working on it will not be forgotten. If it fails, we lose everything, but we're all in it together."

It's a far cry from Hollywood moviemaking. Melina goes to the set in a yellow Fiat. An actor friend's BMW is used by Ellen Burstyn. Melina's longtime companion and makeup artist, Anna, is playing her maid in the film. Her best friend, Despo, is playing her archrival. The budget is modest. Melina calls it *Never on Sunday with Inflation. Never on Sunday* was made for $120,000. The new one will cost $400,000. The production office is downstairs in the apartment building where the Dassins live. Every room in Melina's apartment is used as one of the different sets. Dassin edits each day's footage on an antique Movieola in the basement. One hundred thousand dollars of the budget goes to Ellen Burstyn. Melina and Jules are working for nothing. The risks are high, but so are the rewards.

"We're doing this one for love," says Dassin.

"And," adds Melina triumphantly, "we're doing it for Greece!"

16

LAS VEGAS

Las Vegas, Nevada. Rising like an asteroid of Jello in a desert of some forgotten planet, lit by enough neon to illuminate Chicago at midnight, it survives the rest of the world through pipelines of money and mendacity.

Vegas! It's still there. While the rest of the world reads about the Gilmore execution and the Carter inauguration, the Vegas headlines herald "Playgirls on Ice" above a five-column photo spread of Liberace emerging from a rhinestone Rolls-Royce in a floor-length white mink. It's only Friday night, and I'm not sure I'll survive till Sunday.

Before I get out of the airport, the vulgarity of well-designed decadence hits me between the eyes. Intellectual processes slow to a record crawl as the voice of Totie Fields pierces the din of slot machines: "Please step to the right so those in back of you can pass you on the left." Pregnant women jockey for position with real cowboys in from the ranches, jerking levers and inserting quarters in silent, mocking bandits.

Everybody in Vegas looks like Raquel Welch. You see them, empty-eyed and empty-headed, munching enchiladas at 4 A.M., waiting for taxis in front of the Dunes, hustling drinks at the keno tables, snapping photos at the dinner show at Caesars Palace. They sleep all day and boogie all night, and everybody wants to be Valerie Perrine, who symbolizes the Vegas Vamp, the all-American Dream.

This is the town where everyone's a friend until the bar closes and then everyone's a stranger. It's a plastic paradox where the old begin to live and the young begin to die, and sometimes the tuxedo you rent to get married in turns up three hours later on the corpse at the all-night mortuary ("Go Out in Style at the Permanent Snooze Factory! Emergency Wakes Our Specialty! Credit Cards Welcome!") near the Discreet Motel.

On the way to the MGM Grand Hotel, the cab driver grumbles, "That's the first time I ever turned that corner without waiting in a line of traffic."

"Slow weekend?"

"Ghost City, baby."

They talk like that in Vegas.

At the MGM, there's a contact-lens convention in the Gigi restaurant, a chiropractor's clinic in the Great Caruso room, and Leo the Lion is lying in his cage, facing the wall with humiliation. The pages bombard the speakers of the elevators ("Phone call for Red Buttons"), the swimming pool ("Message for Angie Dickinson") and the MGM theatre, where you can punch a button and order a Tom Collins while you watch a 35-millimeter print of Greta Garbo in *Mata Hari*. I lose two hundred dollars on the nines before dinner. If there's a recession, they didn't hear about it in Vegas.

At the Sahara, Lena Horne and Vic Damone! Lena, undulating, sighing, caressing her songs as if she were snuggling into a feather bed with a good book (or a good friend who's just read one). She purrs rhapsodically "I've Grown Accustomed to Your Face" and every male in the audience still breathing wishes she'd grow accustomed to his. I've seen Lena before, but never like this. She growls. She stalks like a panther in the jungle night.

In her pomegranate jersey, she ties a dinner napkin around her neck to absorb the perspiration, and it looks like a Paris design. She redefines class. And she has never sung better. Along with her new versions of old movie favorites like "A Fine Romance" and "Honeysuckle Rose" (laced with delicious comments on what color the pillars were she leaned on in Technicolor while Red Skelton got the close-ups) she adds a few from films even the buffs can't remember. "Don't remember the movie this one came from—jus' remember some glass scenery," she sighs. The cherry on top of the cake is a medley of twenty-one Richard Rodgers classics with Lena and Vic, less wooden and more mellow than usual and who can blame him on the same stage with the Queen of Pizzazz, swinging their noses off. The polyesters stagger drunkenly to their feet in a rare standing ovation.

Backstage, Lena is dripping water, bundled in terrycloth, trying to phone her daughter Gail Lumet in Hollywood, where Peter Finch, star of Lena's son-in-law Sidney Lumet's *Network*, has just died. "Last thing they need is a nosy mother offerin' condolences before her midnight show," snorts Lena. "Come back at two A.M. and Sammy Davis'll take us out for Chinese breakfast at the Sands." My colon lurches at the thought.

Before I get out of the Sahara, I drop by the lounge to see the career comeback of the famous Mary Kaye Trio. Frank Sinatra and Judy Garland used to pay Mary Kaye just to stay around so they could hear her sing when they got off work. She's got a gal named Nadine Jansen working with her now who plays four keyboards with her left hand while she plays trumpet and flügelhorn with her right hand. Damnedest thing I've ever seen.

She plays like Shorty Rogers, except he needs two hands. She also plays piano like Erroll Garner. No tempo, no rhythm, no style of music eludes this group or gets neglected in their versatile act.

I wake the next afternoon at three—miraculously in my own room back at the MGM. A masseur brings me to life, locating a spot in my left ankle he swears could lead to a dead nerve in my right elbow. Too weak to resist, I am kneaded, pummeled, hacked, slapped and oiled into semiconsciousness in time to lose another two hundred dollars at roulette betting on the nines.

I pass on Tony Orlando and Dawn, sneak by Wayne Newton, and head for the Liberace show at the Hilton International. The room seems bigger than Shea Stadium. An orchestra that sounds as if it were being piped in from Mars beats it daddy eight to the bar while fourteen dancers with white candelabras from something called the Nevada Dance Theater swing onto the stage. The candelabras light up when the lights go out, signaling the arrival of—yes, Virginia, there is a Liberace!

He rides onto the stage in a sequined Rolls, popping out of the back seat in virgin ermine (the only virgin in Vegas, no doubt) with chubby fingers weighted with diamonds. His tux is a trapezoid of silver sequins as he steps to a piano made of mirrors on a stage filled with lighted Christmas trees. During "Winter Wonderland" the ceiling opens up and it literally snows all over the stage, the piano and Liberace, whose teeth match all the ivory keys of his piano. As he shifts into a snappy "Skater's Waltz," the back of the stage opens up to reveal the internationally famous—yes, it's the Dancing Waters! Direct from Somewhere! They turn green, they turn blue and red, too! The whole stage looks like somebody threw up after eating a banana split.

Liberace looks like Mary Margaret McBride and sounds like a cross between Tallulah Bankhead and Truman Capote. But there's no time for laughter. "Lee" is about to "slip into something more spectacular." A voice like God parting the Red Sea announces: "And now . . . the Palace of Versailles proudly presents . . . Frédéric Chopin!" Yes, it's Lee, dressed like Cornel Wilde, in a blue-sequined tux dripping with French lace, playing the "Polonaise" while fountains of turquoise water splash recklessly behind him in a drawing room filled with ballet dancers and crystal chandeliers. He can't top this! But wait. There's more.

Lee, in high-heeled sequined boots, plays boogie-woogie eight to the bar, then sixteen to the bar, in a brand-new mink, lined in red, with all the faces of the little minks writhing in a mask of revulsion. Maybe they don't like boogie-woogie. Maybe they don't like Las Vegas. "Remember that bank I used to cry all the way to?" beams Lee, undaunted. "Well, I bought it."

Then he brings out his chauffeur, who plays "Slaughter on Tenth Avenue," and a fifteen-year-old protégée, who sings like Edith Piaf. But enough of all that music. It's time to show the ring collection. Lee, in Black Diamond mink lined in Austrian rhinestones, bends over to the fainting women from Des Moines on a night out from the Midwest Dr Pepper Bottling Convention, and shows the rings on every finger—Russian sapphires, diamonds in the shape of pianos and candlesticks, and a watch of twenty-six rubies with two diamonds you press releasing a fly-open top that reveals the time in star sapphires!

Can I go now? No! It's time for the red-white-and-blue Rolls convertible with a license that reads "88 Keys" from which emerges—you guessed it—in a red-white-and-blue Mardi Gras costume enshrouded with white maribou feathers. The lights go out while the band strikes up "Stars and Stripes Forever," Lee lights up in firecrackers and Roman candles, and then flies across the ceiling, screaming "Mary Poppins, eat your heart out!" The audience, limp from hysteria, eats it like milk and cookies. It's awful. It's over. Outside, the chauffeur is signing autographs and selling Liberace records while a loudspeaker rages: "Telephone call for Shecky Greene."

No, I don't want to bump and grind till 4 A.M. in the underground Benihana Palace.

I'm too weary to catch Ann-Margret, too bruised to enter the $100,000 bingo game at 3 A.M. at the Aladdin, too broke to place another five-dollar bet on the nines at the Circus Circus while trapeze acts fly over my head at 5 A.M. as nude go-go girls feed me a champagne breakfast.

The plane leaves the ground. The lights blaze below, scorching the moon surface with an electric bill that would pay off the national debt. The man next to me beams. "Love that town! Won ten thousand dollars on the nines." Is manslaughter legal at 30,000 feet?

17

MARSHA MASON

MARSHA MASON IS A MISSING PERSON. ON-SCREEN, SHE NEVER FAILS to make an impression. Acrylic smile, trapezoid mouth, funny-valentine lips curving down at the sides like a child's Crayola drawing, eyes bubbling on the verge of tears. But when the makeup is packed away and the dressing room locked, Marsha Mason disappears. Even the fan magazines are scratching their featherheads. Nobody has a clue. We haven't exactly been stampeded with a plethora of Marsha Mason interviews. On the New York hotel register, she's listed as Marsha Simon. The press agent from her new movie *The Good-bye Girl*, in which she once again lights up the screen as a warm, huggable, over-the-hill chorus girl with a precocious daughter and an army of fruitcake boyfriends who march through her heart like Grant taking Richmond, emerges from an elevator to inform anyone who asks that there is no Marsha Mason on the floors above.

The sunny, sweet-tempered, talkative gal who signs for room-service chicken salad and iced tea writes "Mrs. Neil Simon" on the check. The waiter looks puzzled, shrugs, and leaves. Even the staff is convinced no movie star is staying here. "I was Marsha Mason four years ago," says the girl who made headlines when she married the world's funniest playwright. "But I've been Mrs. Neil Simon ever since. He is the star in the family and the rest of it is unimportant to me. There are reasons why I don't do interviews. There hasn't been a lot I've done that people have been interested in. Mine is not one of those across-the-board success stories. Also, people never seem to remember me from one film to another." Neil Simon says she spends three hours in front of a mirror making herself look homely. She has no idea how attractive she is. Marsha laughs. "Streisand has an extremely clear image of herself. Such a thing just never occurred to me. When I step in front of a camera, whatever comes out that day is what you get. I have no image. And I like it. To be a Streisand, or a Jack Nicholson, or a Robert Redford—to have that kind of mass appeal—I couldn't cope with that."

Despite the chaos and the jumbled never-never-land values of a plastic world like Hollywood, she is adamant about one thing: "I want a career that is interesting and fulfilling, yet at the same time we have a private life that is normal. We have a cardinal rule. We don't do any interviews at home. We tried it once and the writer printed a story about our neighbor across the street, Henry Fonda. It's crazy enough out there already, with Gray Line bus tours through the front yard and I can't get home at night because three thousand tourists are in the street photographing Dean Martin's house. We try to stay sane in an insane environment."

Is she Betty Boop or Betty Crocker? Until four years ago, she was just plain Nutsy Fagan. Born in St. Louis to strict Catholic parents, she "grew up with so many rose-colored glasses on I didn't lose my virginity until I was in my twenties." Her father was a failed printer who ended up working for the Department of Vehicles ("something to do with license plates") and it took seven years of analysis to work out her feelings of suppression and guilt. She moved to New York in 1964 after four years of college, worked as a clerk for the New York Central Railroad, married an actor named Gary Campbell "out of a need to feel an attachment to somebody—we were both scared and lonely," and spent most of her time shuffling in and out of TV commercials with migraines. "It was a weaning period. We were both growing and learning, but I needed to stretch my wings." A role in the national tour of *Cactus Flower* led to two movies (*Blume in Love* and *Cinderella Liberty*) and a divorce. "I was floundering and full of anger. I was twenty-seven, married, divorced, in therapy, and my father was still asking me, 'Are you being a nice girl?' The actors I met were either getting horrible divorces or they were homosexuals. I sort of gave up on ever having a mature relationship."

Enter a cherubic, balding playwright with horn-rimmed glasses named Neil Simon, who had been married to his wife Joan for twenty years when she suddenly and tragically died of cancer, leaving him with a desk full of hollow jokes and two daughters to raise. Marsha had deserted a good, steady, well-paying job on the soap opera "Love of Life" and was working hard in a San Francisco production of *Private Lives* when her agent rushed her back to New York to read for a new Neil Simon play called *The Good Doctor*. She was bone weary, had no hope of getting the part, didn't want it anyway, kept thinking about moving to Los Angeles. The playwright stuck his head in and said, "Aren't you the girl from *Love in Bloom*?" Getting the name of the movie backward made her laugh. She didn't discover until later that in the blackness of the empty theater where she was reading for the role she was "only a page and a half into the script when he leaned over to the director and whispered 'Hire her!' He says now that he remembered me from a Manufacturers Hanover Trust commercial that always played right in the middle of the Knicks game. It was just one of those extraordinary chemical things. On the first day of rehearsals, we were all sitting around this table reading the script aloud. We took a coffee break. He came around, put his hand on my shoulder, and I remember patting his hand with my hand like we were old friends. I can't explain it. It all sounds so silly. I was very embarrassed. We were married twenty-one days later."

It was like one of those comic slogans hanging over an analyst's couch: "Today is the first day of the rest of your life!" Marsha was like one of those leading ladies in B movies who wake up in somebody else's bed, wearing somebody else's clothes, with somebody else's passport. "I could understand it," she says reflectively, "if I had been actively looking but I had already made up my mind to devote myself to my career. I was in a Broadway show, I had two movies under my belt, I didn't need marriage or security. But I felt it was right. I just let myself go. Here was a man with growing children who were going through heavy changes, and I was a new wife with a ready-made family and responsibilities I never dreamed of, but they were so wonderful they made it easy. I decided to play it by ear and use my instincts. It was the girls who suggested we get married. I knew I couldn't replace their mother, but they said, 'Why don't you come and live with us—we won't tell our friends you're not married!' I had played it safe long enough and I knew what that was like. It was time to find out what a relationship was like."

The play was a flop, but Marsha got an Oscar nomination for *Cinderella Liberty*. "We were getting married, I was sitting in New York with a whole new family, getting ready to move to California into a brand-new house. I was so nervous I went out and overdosed on hamburgers, malts and junk food, ended up with a gall bladder attack, and got the news about the Oscar nomination in a hospital room. That's when I made the decision that a career wasn't worth it. After we were married, Neil confessed to me he hated actresses. One day he announced: 'OK, this isn't going to work—either give up your career or me!' I thought for a moment, and said, 'OK, I'll give up the career!' I think he was floored. He was so stunned by Joan's death that he was afraid of being left alone again. So I decided to commit myself to him totally and for the first time in my life I have all of my priorities in the right place. Ironically, at the same time he said, 'You can't work again!' he turned around and wrote two movies for me to act in."

Moving to California, she says, gave them both the fresh start they needed to build a life on an equal level. He plays tennis, feels physically active, is writing more and better than ever. His new play, *Chapter Two*, which opens December 4 on Broadway, is "very autobiographical, about a second marriage, readjustment and letting go." Marsha's career is jumping. She was a great success in a Los Angeles stage production of *The Heiress* last year, and finished three movies in a row: *Audrey Rose*, in which she played the hysterical mother of a reincarnated child, *The Good-bye Girl,* and the forthcoming Neil Simon parody of Bogart crime melodramas called *The Cheap Detective*. She likes the latter two, frowns with crinkled disdain at the mention of *Audrey Rose*. "I cried my eyes out in every scene. There were so many tears it was like a Greek tragedy, except that without a character to work with, I ended up being ultimately boring." In *The Cheap Detective* she plays a combination of Claire Trevor, Gladys George and Gloria Grahame—"one of those maniacal, desperate, supportive women who never get the guy. I wear a blond-floozie wig, long eyelashes and look wonderfully cheap and trashy!" In *The Good-bye Girl* she found working with Richard Dreyfuss like "hitching myself to a skyrocket. He carries most of the comic thrust of the movie. I'm the one who had to root the movie in reality. I was always stirring spaghetti and telling the kid to go to bed, and what I really wanted to do was act crazy, too. We read it aloud for Neil and he said we were better than the script, so he threw out sixty pages and started all over again. It proves his philosophy that if the story isn't strong, you're only as good as your last joke."

All of which still, amazingly, leaves plenty of time for a balanced homelife. "It was a big adjustment for two New Yorkers who were trained to move in a certain rhythm, but life in California has given us peace. I got tired of the kids getting mugged for the lunch money on their way to school in Manhattan. We get sick of the interminable sunshine in California, but I have a vegetable garden, fruit trees, two dogs and a cat. I'm reading up on canning. I get up in the morning and go down and cut some roses for the house. I like being back in New York, but I'm worried about my avocado trees. Neil has a separate office next to a sports club where he can look out from his typewriter and watch Jimmy Connors playing tennis."

Her unfulfilled fantasy is still to sing opera, but meanwhile she's just directed her first film for the American Film Institute—a twenty-five-minute dramatization on videotape of the seduction scene from *The Good Doctor*. "They give you a thousand dollars and you're on your own. It costs that much for food bills for the crew, so naturally you end up spending your own money. But now I have to go back and learn how to edit it. I still talk too much, but the best thing about my life now is that whatever I do, I've learned to do it with a sense of humor about myself."

It's Mrs. Neil Simon who ushers me out, but it's Marsha Mason who giggles happily when the door closes.

18

JACQUELINE BISSET

(1)

LONDON. JACQUELINE BISSET, THE MOVIES' GOLDEN GIRL, HAS MADE a career out of swimming through shallow roles into tanks of public attention, but after thirty films in ten years, she's finally making her first comedy. It's called *Someone Is Killing the Great Chefs of Europe* and every scene is about food. "I can't even look at a poached egg," says Jackie, who prefers smoking to eating and ferrets her way through two packs a day between takes. "In one scene, they spent three thousand dollars on fish.

"At one point, George Segal and I had to eat seventeen pigeons *en croûte*. Every time we broke the crust we had to replace it. One pigeon *en croûte* is a two-page recipe that takes two days to prepare. We had thirty-one of them, individually prepared by Paul Bocuse, the famous French chef. I finally turned to George and said, 'If we don't get this right, they'll make us eat every goddam one of them!'

We stopped after seventeen and I swear I never want to look at another pigeon as long as I live!"

The movie, written by Peter Stone and directed by Canada's Ted Kotcheff, is a comedy thriller centered around a banquet for Queen Elizabeth to which the great chefs of Europe have been summoned to prepare their gastronomic specialties. Each is mysteriously murdered in a culinary style befitting his favorite dish, although Jackie, as the world's top dessert chef, is narrowly saved by George Segal, her ex-husband, a fast-food entrepreneur who prefers Big Macs to bouillabaisse.

"I can't even make a pie crust," winks Jackie, "and I have to make a strawberry bombe big enough for the Chinese army to eat." So much for authenticity. Yet, she made *The Deep* without knowing how to swim, and played a very famous widow of an assassinated United States President who marries a Greek shipping magnate in *The Greek Tycoon* without ever meeting Jackie Onassis. As one wag comments: "She's had a lot of experience working with inanimate objects on film, such as an underwater shipwreck and Charles Bronson."

Filming has been in Munich, Venice, Paris and London, and the elaborate sets have included locations in the top four-star restaurants of four countries. "The queen wouldn't let us use the kitchen of Buckingham Palace, so we substituted the Lido nightclub instead."

Half-French and raised in England, the emerald-eyed star says she took the movie even though it meant being away from home and working seventeen hours a day during the Christmas holidays because "I've played so many clinging, frightened women who stood around in bad movies as decorations that I thought it was about time I proved I could handle a comedy. It's quite pleasant to be able to smile for a change. Usually I ask the director if I might ease a grin in here or there, and they say, 'No, we want you sultry and scared to death.' Well, I've played so many victims that I can do it standing on my head. Every script I get gives me the feeling I've done it already. This one was a real challenge. I saw Ted Kotcheff's last film, *Fun with Dick and Jane*. I didn't like it. But I did like this part. I haven't done a comedy since *Le Magnifique* with Jean-Paul Belmondo in Paris. It was a bomb in America, but I did that one, too, because it was fun."

Although Bisset has a reputation for "taking on any movie if it has six good lines in it," she's in a reflective stage these days. Her four-year love affair with a younger man, Moroccan Jewish clothes designer Victor Drai, is flourishing. Victor has given up haute couture to sell real estate in Beverly Hills and the couple have a fourteen-room Benedict Canyon hacienda once owned by Clark Gable where they more or less spend most of their time together when Jackie isn't off pacing the world in exotic movie locations.

"I get a lot of scripts offered me, but they come at different times. Most actresses get an offer and ask two questions: Who's writing it? and Who's directing it? I only ask one: Can I stand to go away again? Am I going to spend three boring months somewhere, or am I going to learn something? I don't live for my work, but if I'm going to work I want to get something out of it."

What she got out of *The Greek Tycoon* was thirty-six costumes by Halston, but she defensively adds that "after so much nasty publicity, I think most people will be surprised at how good that movie is going to be. I think we took a trashy subject and turned it into something better than anticipated. I like Anthony Quinn. I don't flourish on a film unless I feel protected. There has to be a mutual liking. It's terribly important for me to feel confident. This is not a business you do on your own, and I give more of myself if I feel an affection from the people I'm working with. I've had a good working experience on most films. I haven't always liked the films, but I've enjoyed doing most of them. Just coping with my fear of water in *The Deep* changed my life. That was a wonderful experience, although it was the hardest thing I've ever done physically. That film damn near killed me. I always think of myself as a complete coward. When it came out, I was already in Greece doing *The Greek Tycoon*, so I missed all the fuss. I never read one review. It has made an immense fortune, but I'll never see a penny of it."

Money, she says, is not important. Victor gave her a black Rolls-Royce and she won't even drive it. Still, it would be nice to experience solvency. "The only film I ever had a percentage deal on was *Day for Night* and Truffaut never paid me a nickel. But I feel positive about my life and I want to go on playing positive, contributing women. My work is improving enormously as a result of the films I'm doing now. It's impossible to save money. I bought my house seven years ago and I love it with a passion, but I'm only home long enough to pay bills. Because of my dual citizenship, the taxes are enormous. I live simply by Hollywood standards. My house has beams, fireplaces and tile floors. No gold lamé or marble columns or Japanese gardeners.

"I suppose if I got married, we could file joint tax returns and save money, but I don't believe in marriage or children. I have nothing to contribute as a wife or mother and those labels would put me in a box and ruin a perfectly beautiful relationship. So I trudge on, looking for something meaningful to do. I'm having an absolutely gorgeous time playing a goofball, but this film has been total confusion for me. We couldn't get home for Christmas. I had no time to buy Christmas presents. I don't know where my mail is. I'm probably the only movie star in the world who didn't get a single Christmas card this year."

It was time to reenter the world of sliced, boned, grated, sautéed, minced, pureed, whipped, chopped and seasoned cinematic haute cuisine. "I hope I never see another duck à l'orange," she sighed, ducking a flying eggplant as her zany co-stars began their arduous task of preparing, eating and throwing the day's edible props at each other. "And," she added with a soupçon of twinkling mischief in her million-dollar boudoir eyes, "I hope the next film I do takes place in Beverly Hills."

(2)

LONDON. It is 7:30 A.M. in the velvet-drenched Café Royal near Piccadilly Circus, and Robert Morley, the hippo-shaped British character comedian, sits staring glassily at bowls of iced prawns, a side of beef Wellington, an entire baby lamb trussed in paper panties, a roast suckling pig, an entire hog's head stuffed with apples and chestnuts, six lobsters, platters of pastrami, salvers of smoked salmon, twenty-four stuffed artichokes, thirty-six oysters, cornucopias of pineapples, grapes, tartes and crepes, wheels of cheese, terrines of pâté, silver sidecars laden with strudels, apricot puddings, raspberries and flaming floating islands. Mr. Morley looks ill.

A look of supreme joy mixed with gastronomical panic floods his face. Several unprintable tons of porcine pulchritude lurch forward and he falls over dead, his head smashing into a fountain of whipped cream. It's his suicide breakfast and Mr. Morley, you see, has just eaten himself to death. All in good fun, naturally, since it's all part of a big climactic scene for a new movie called *Someone Is Killing the Great Chefs of Europe.* "This makes the banquet scene from *Tom Jones* look like a Depression breadline," jokes the jovial, rotund Morley while a makeup artist wipes crushed strawberries from his grinning face. "What do you mean, do it again?"

Ted Kotcheff needs another take. So Mr. Morley starts eating again. He sits, stunned from the sheer volume of his gluttony—bloated, comatose. Suddenly his eyes pop open, a look of surprise on his face, and he belches. Then his great head smashes again into the strawberries Romanoff. Kotcheff says, "Print it!" and Mr. Morley goes off for a prebreakfast Alka-Seltzer. The scene is total chaos in the elegant old restaurant of kings and highwaymen that dates back to Queen Victoria. The Café Royal was Oscar Wilde's favorite restaurant, which seems fittingly ghostly, since Morley once played Wilde in a movie about his life. But the gold-encrusted dining room had never witnessed such madness as on this day of moviemaking lunacy.

Italian, French, German, English and American crews were shifting tables, ordering waiters around, disconnecting lamps, rearranging menus in four different languages. "Hurry up!" shouted Kotcheff. "This place looks like a suburban pizzeria! Besides, we gotta be outta here by four-thirty so they can open up for their regular dinner business." Kotcheff is under constant pressure to finish on time, because the movie had a deadline to meet in order to qualify for German tax-shelter financing. Once the investment is used, then there's no more money. It's an American film, but the interiors have been shot in Munich and the food locations have included the famous Maxim's and Tour d'Argent restaurants in Paris as well as the fish market in Venice, Italy. "With fifty-two shooting days in four countries in the dead of winter when you only get two hours of sun a day, it's been one of the most difficult films ever made," says star George Segal. "Exhausting and chaotic. I don't think any director except Ted Kotcheff could've done it."

Segal worked for Kotcheff on *Fun with Dick and Jane,* so they are old friends. And Kotcheff seems perfect for the assignment. He's a gourmand and comes from a family of restaurant owners. "There's food and eating and cooking in every scene in the film," he says. "There's even a food fight between two chefs in which brains, livers, sweetbreads and mushy foods are thrown all over everybody." Before Kotcheff exploded on the film scene with his highly praised Canadian film *The Apprenticeship of Duddy Kravitz*, he used to hang around his father's restaurant in Toronto. He also had an uncle who owned a wholesale slaughterhouse and weighed 390 pounds. The uncle, he swears to Segal's co-star Jacqueline Bisset, once ate twenty-six lamb chops for breakfast. When the cast of *Someone Is Killing the Great Chefs of Europe* isn't eating and cooking in front of the camera, they tell food stories.

"This is a seven-million-dollar movie," says Jackie Bisset, "and twenty thousand dollars has been spent on food. We're all watching our weight like crazy, but it's not as difficult as you think. You can't eat the props. It's like working in an ice cream parlor. If you're surrounded by food all day, you end up eating a green salad. When I'm not working, I usually put on ten pounds just eating potatoes." Kotcheff, who loves food, has actually lost weight. "I'm in such a hurry to finish the picture and move all this equipment and all these people from one continent to the other that I'm burning up all my calories in nervous energy. I gained fifteen pounds researching the three-star restaurants. Now I've lost my appetite. It's a great way to diet."

The movie itself, billed as "the delicious comedy," is about a divorced couple (Segal and Bisset) who are opposed on both personal and professional levels. He thinks his fast-food franchises, called the Humpty Dumpty Omelette Shops, are the answer to the workingman's prayer, while she shivers at the thought of processed foods and instant chemical concentrates. He's happy with a cheeseburger; she's Julia Child with sex appeal and also the most famous pastry chef in the world. Robert Morley is a one-man combination of Egon Ronay, Lucius Beebe and the *Guide Michelin*—a powerful restaurant critic and editor of *Epicure* magazine. When Jackie arrives in London to prepare her famous bombe Richelieu for the queen under Morley's aegis, she runs into Segal, who is setting up his omelette chain. The fireworks fly, and so do the murders, as the great chefs of Europe are found dead in comic situations relating to their specialties. In London, the greatest chef from Buckingham Palace is baked in his own oven. In Venice, the Italian master of lobster aragosta is found drowned in his own lobster tank. The greatest epicurean master of France, whose pressed duck is a legend, is crushed in his own duck press. Jackie Bisset is next. Her strawberry bombe has a bomb in it. "I actually had to prepare this enormous dessert," giggles the glamorous star. "I never even made a pie crust in my life."

George Segal is the only cast member who has nothing to do with food. "Next to a Sabrett hot dog off the street with mustard and sauerkraut," he says, "there is nothing better. I don't know anything about food and couldn't care less. I believe in diners, where the truck drivers eat. If there's a big turnover, you know it's fresh."

Calorie-conscious moviegoers addicted to liquid protein should be warned in advance. This is not on the weight-watcher's recommended list. Comedy screenwriter Peter Stone has been dining out on the subject for two years. "It's a whodunit," he confides, "but food is the star. There haven't been many American movies about food. Americans are obsessed with eating, yet we're eating more and more junk food. The food in this movie will be haute cuisine."

Apart from the staggering array of culinary sights in the film, some of the great chefs of Europe in real life have been employed to play themselves. Michael Chow, of Mr. Chow's gourmet Chinese restaurants in London and Beverly Hills, will guest star, and Paul Bocuse, the most famous French chef of them all, designed the menus and supervised the food, which includes such mouth-watering wonders as *entrecôte à la Mirabeau*, lobster with artichokes, roast venison *au poivre* and veal scallop Massenet.

Most of this bacchanalian feast will be consumed by poor Robert Morley, who plays the chief murder suspect in the movie. "I'm just perfect for the part," he twinkles impishly, sucking a pheasant bone. "When God made me, he said, 'Let's make something special.' Don't ask me how much I weigh. To tell you the truth, I haven't the foggiest idea, but I didn't once have a play specially written for me called *Hippo Dancing* for nothing. I don't own a bathroom scale, but I do have the perfect vital statistics—fifty-fifty-fifty!" To make certain Mr. Morley and the other eaters don't look unnecessarily gross, director Kotcheff has hired John Alcott, the masterful cinematographer who, after photographing Stanley Kubrick's *Clockwork Orange* and *2001: A Space Odyssey*, won an Academy Award for making *Barry Lyndon* look so beautiful. George Segal says enthusiastically: "No comedy has ever looked like this. The food is shot in soft lighting like Vermeer paintings. Jackie Bisset and I are having so much fun, we're trying to find another script to do together. Even I look breathtaking. This is my Ryan O'Neal look."

It's time for the scene to be shot from a different angle. This time, Jackie Bisset and George Segal are inserted into the long shot, biting into a fifty-pound cake. "I don't know one single successful movie star who ever had a happy childhood," says Segal. "I'm having one now." When the movie is finished and the public gets a look at Segal and Bisset reaching their boiling point, the recipe will serve a projected fifty million viewers. "It might not be a work of art," says one observer, "but it's gotta be tasty."

19

LUCILLE BALL

LUCILLE BALL LEANS AGAINST HER BACKGAMMON TABLE AND SIPS her second afternoon Scotch in the quiet hush of her Beverly Hills home. No reason to hurry. Her kids have grown up and moved away. Her husband, Gary Morton, is dining out with golf buddies.

A California sunset casts an orange glow across the empty swimming pool outside, reminding her it will soon be night, time to slash on some lipstick and drive with a visiting sister-in-law from New York to a nearby restaurant for an early steak before bedtime. An old dog with asthma wheezes on a chintz sofa. Ice cubes melt lazily in her glass. The only sounds of life in the rambling old house. She's alone, but she's not lonely.

There are no cameras turning, no signs of makeup men and hairdressers. The lines in her face have been honestly earned, along with the millions she's made being the idol of millions. Tonight she doesn't have to be the star of "I Love Lucy." She's just a woman, a mother, a wife with the night off who doesn't have to be "on."

After twenty-five years as the funniest woman in America, she can look at the TV scripts that line the walls of her den and know it didn't happen by accident.

Is she happy with the way things turned out? She smiles wryly and runs her hands through her Popsicle-orange hair. "How could I be anything else? The CBS tribute I did before Christmas and the accolades that flooded in from the industry just floored me."

In addition to those from William Paley and the CBS brass, the cables are still pouring in. She fingers them proudly. "John Wayne, Gale Gordon, Sammy Davis, Junior, Bob Hope, Tennessee Ernie Ford, Carol Burnett, my writers, my sponsors, the people who did all of my lab work. Here's one from Vivian Vance that says, 'A wise man once said hitch your wagon to a star, and I did. You made me what I am today, and I am satisfied. Love, Viv.' She hated being called Ethel, you know. But she was a great show doctor and a wonderful right arm and when she got married and moved East and quit the show, I never really did recover."

Awards? "They meant something because they were all sincere. I haven't had that many. I've had plenty, but not a plethora. I couldn't do a whole house in them, but I could do a small room."

It's all over now. The Lucy shows have moved out, making way for headier stuff. The nineteen *TV Guide* covers she was on are all framed on the wall of her pool house. Her scrapbooks are as full as her memories, and she doesn't look back with any regrets on her reign for a quarter of a century as the queen of television.

"I keep up with my old TV family. Viv calls me all the time and we all exchange gifts at Christmas. I find myself watching old reruns and enjoying them for the first time, because when I did them I had to look at rushes and be critical and I never saw the finished shows with music and sound effects. Some of them I've never seen. My writers were the best in the business. None of those shows were ad-libbed. Everything was planned, rehearsed and timed. The years those writers put in and the way every comedy series has stolen from them for the past twenty years . . . it makes me sick to think they never got an Emmy. We had a winner as long as it lasted.

"The secret, I think, was reality. My audiences saw their own foibles mirrored in what happened to Lucy. They could watch and say, 'Oh, Mabel, that's what happened when you baked your first cake, remember?' We squeezed comedy out of vacuum cleaners, washing machines, grocery bills. Now the world is ugly and the comedy is ugly, too. After the six-o'clock news, nothing that follows is very funny. On 'I Love Lucy' we never married the homosexual uncle to another man in the living room or electrocuted the children in the bathtub or drowned the grandfather in chicken soup. The things you see now are horrifying, and you're supposed to laugh at them. I don't understand it, and I don't think I ever will, and it certainly isn't entertainment.

"But times have changed and we expect more. I'll give you an example of how even I am guilty. One night a few years ago I was flipping the dial looking for a show called 'Combat,' and I finally found it and settled back to watch. These soldiers in camouflage helmets were creeping through the jungle, and nothing was happening. They were just creeping. Very boring, I thought.

"Finally a shot rang out and a guy's head rolled right in front of the camera, and I thought, Good heavens! and then nothing else happened for a long time and I finally said, 'All right, awreddy—what's with this director?' I was looking at the real war in Vietnam and didn't know it. Real blood, real bullets, real guys getting killed, and I was complaining because there wasn't enough action! Today we're satiated with violence and sharks and sex, and we just accept it. It's sad for the young people because they have nothing to look forward to."

What does she watch for laughs? "Nothing much. Nancy Walker is funny, she just doesn't have my writers. 'All in the Family' put words like *dago, wop, kike* back into our vocabulary and taught little kids that if they got a laugh in their living room they'd work even better in the street. I don't watch 'Mary Hartman,' either. I send money to aid V.D. clinics, why should I look to them for laughs?"

Yet despite the offers she's had to bring back the Lucy shows, she says she "knew when to throw in the towel. It was traumatic to close down the arena, lock up the offices and get rid of all those people who worked for me so many years. I cried for four months. I miss the creativity, I miss Vivian, I miss the friends. For twenty-five years, it was like going to a party.

"When Desi and I were beginning to have serious trouble with our marriage, we couldn't quit because we were committed to CBS for five-year stretches. Sometimes I was happier on the show than I was at home. But if we were coming out today with our first Lucy show, we'd be hooted off the network. The generations of kids I baby-sat for with my show are now my loyal fans, but if we started over now they'd howl, 'Where's the sex, where's the violence, where are the sick jokes?'

"I've always prided myself in knowing when to get off and I think I waited three years too long. I was ready to quit five years before I did. I was getting too old to be yelled at by Uncle Harry for doing idiotic things. Nobody twisted my arm but myself."

She is deluged with letters, calls, wires from people begging her to go back on the air with "decent entertainment," but she firmly believes you "can't go back again. I can't believe just doing the Lucy show again would cure all the ills of the world. They're buying tickets and lining up to see sex and violence, and the new generation is already sullied by hopelessness. There's no going back for them. Linda Lovelace is a celebrity, for God's sake! If Walt Disney was alive, he might have some answers. I don't."

The sound of children playing on a neighbor's lawn reminds her to knock on wood about her own. At a time when most show-biz parents didn't know what their kids were up to, she was a strict parent who always knew where hers were. "I still know where they are because they call and tell me. Luci and Desi, Junior, have their own homes but they never really got away from me because I'm the original Jewish mother, which is a helluva compliment. After all, I'm Jewish by marriage. I'm also a perfectionist. Both terms are almost dirty words today."

So many stars turn out miserable, but Lucy ran a business like a lady tycoon, soared to the top of television and raised a family all at the same time and always landed on her feet, like a cat falling off the top of a refrigerator. What's her secret? "If you asked me that a few years back, I couldn't answer because I was in the throes of disaster. But I met a very unusual man, and there aren't many like him. Gary Morton brought back all the dreams I had thrown away.

"I have a lot to thank many people for, but to find at such a late date someone who had lived, who wasn't looking around the corner for someone younger and prettier, who knew how to enjoy a home, who was anxious to learn and build and live and love and take the bad with the good—well, it saved my life.

"It took me a few years into the marriage to realize I had made this great choice, but he's an unusual man and he's made me unusually happy. He came at a tough time and got my kids through their difficult teen-age years. He was a great stepfather and a great husband to a wife who was the big star. I had already seen how tough it was for a man in my previous marriage. It wasn't easy for Desi. They called him a Cuban bongo player. They didn't know what a great businessman he was. Well, nobody knew what a great guy Gary was, either.

"He sat for five years watching and learning. He didn't get a title and he didn't do anything on my show for a long time. He was just 'the star's husband.' But I'm a great believer in nepotism, you know. I had my sister producing my show, both husbands always worked with me, my kids were both on the show, my brother was on salary. If they can cut the mustard, they're in.

"I never lived for the Joneses. When Desi and I divorced, it was like the desecration of the Bible. I even heard from the Catholic Church. I was in a dilemma. It was Dr. Norman Vincent Peale who straightened me out. He said, 'You must do what's right for you, and then everything else will fall into place,' and that's when I learned I couldn't live my life for thousands of others."

By accident, the redhead from Jamestown, New York, who got fired from every job in show business had landed in Hollywood as a Goldwyn Girl. Her climb was tough, but she carved a dazzling career out of pride and the determination to survive. She's earned a good rest.

"I took mud pies in the face, danced in the chorus of Fred Astaire pictures, played second banana to Red Skelton, but I did what I was told and never squawked because I was learning my craft.

"Today, they want to be instant stars. I made loads of films, but I never really made it the easy way. TV made me what I am today. Now I'll find something else to do. I still have a commitment to do two specials a year for CBS, but I want to take some time off. Vegas? I'm not a stand-up comic. I never could sing, though I tried in *Mame*. Since I broke my leg, I can't dance like I used to, either, because I can't bounce back. Broadway? Never again. If you're in a flop, they kill you. If you're in a hit, you're stuck forever. Broadway isn't what it used to be. It doesn't mean that much anymore.

"I still get movie scripts, but I don't have to do what Bette Davis does. I won't play hatchet murderesses. I'm at the age when I don't have to live up to any image. I don't have to be on at parties. I get together with the old-timers from MGM and we relive funny anecdotes about the USO tours, but I'm no good at one-liners and I don't know any jokes. I'll surface somewhere."

She sips her Scotch and watches the moon rise over her sculptured lawn, and you wouldn't know it was Lucille Ball. "The hardest thing about 'I Love Lucy' was coming in the same door every Monday with the same people and wiping out everything that happened the week before. To this day, I can't tell you what I did yesterday, but," she adds, eyes twinkling with the old moxie, "I know what I'd like to do tomorrow."

20

JIMMY STEWART

LONDON. JIMMY STEWART AT SEVENTY IS, SHUCKS, PRETTY MUCH like an old man playing Jimmy Stewart at twenty. "Well—uh—c'mon in, your tea's gettin' cold." The drawl, even in the formality of a Victorian drawing room at the stuffy old Connaught Hotel, is the same drawl that stopped Harvey in his tracks and got Mr. Smith to Washington. The gangly walk has slowed to a septuagenarian shuffle now, but Jimmy Stewart is moving right along. "My heart's in good shape, knock on wood. Duke Wayne's had cancer, Hank Fonda had a heart attack, and Walter Pidgeon is recovering from a blood clot on the brain, but I just keep rollin' along like Ol' Man River."

Right now he's rollin' through London, playing a small part in a new movie remake of *The Big Sleep*, the Forties private-eye melodrama immortalized by Bogart and Bacall. "When you come right down to it, it's a cameo, or whatever they call these roles old actors get to keep going. I play a sick old general who calls in Robert

Mitchum because I'm being blackmailed. Sarah Miles and Candy Clark play my two daughters. It's just a day and a half of work, and then I'm on my way home. I don't believe in remakes and it isn't much of a part, but I like to keep a finger in the pie. There isn't much work for an old codger like me back home."

Home is still Hollywood, where Jimmy and Gloria Stewart live on a tree-lined street next door to Lucille Ball, but you're likely to find this survivor of forty-five years in show business (he's never had an acting lesson) anywhere on the Rand-McNally the work takes him. Somehow he has miraculously managed to plow through the mud of changing social values with blinders on ("Just like a mule," he grins), symbolizing solidarity, reliability, apple pie and the American way of life. It is not surprising that his next movie role will be in a new Lassie movie with Mickey Rooney.

At seventy, he just turned down his first offer to do a porno film, and when he tells it, he scratches his white hair and looks plumb baffled, like Huck Finn getting his first look at the wide Missouri. "I tried to play a villain once, in 1935, in *After the Thin Man*. It's the only time I ever played a murderer and the audience laughed me off the screen. I've been playing Jimmy Stewart ever since. Now if I turned up in one of those porno things, if I were a member of the audience I'd ask, 'What in the hell is Stewart trying to prove?' It's a long time between roles because I've got the old image to live with. Kate Hepburn will go on forever because she can go from movies to the stage and back again. But she's a special case. Most of us don't get offered anything. They're just not writing the roles."

If the role is in London, he's likely to take it. His daughter lives there and London audiences have always greeted him with open arms. "I played here recently for seven months in *Harvey*. I hadn't played London for twenty-five years. Whenever everything else fails, I can always drag out ol' *Harvey*. I've played in that so many times that white rabbit has become part of my life. Whenever I feel blue, I turn around and *Harvey*'s always there. I'm touring Australia next year with Mildred Natwick in *Harvey*, but Helen Hayes told me to just stop calling her, she's just sick and tired of *Harvey*.

"I'm very superstitious and I talk to myself a lot, just like Elwood P. Dowd. I can be in a crowd of folks or waiting for a plane and a man will come up to me and he's shabbily dressed and he's been hittin' the booze, see—he'll say, 'Jim, is Harvey with you?' I turn around and he's not smiling. This is no joke. I say, 'No, he's home with a cold,' and the guy will say, 'Well, give him my best regards.' It's happened many, many times."

With or without *Harvey*, the Stewarts are hitting the road more these days than they did when Jimmy was a big star. "Now that the kids have moved away and left us with a big, empty house in Beverly Hills, we think more about what we're gonna do than we did before. Gloria is head of the World Wildlife Fund and the East African Wildlife Federation, so we travel a lot. We're planning a trip to the Antarctic soon. But I've never felt like retiring. I had pneumonia in May, but it was nothing serious."

His talk is as slow as his sips of English tea. There are moments when his hands shake, especially when he talks about the "good old days," and at times it's an even bet as to whether he'll get to the end of a sentence. "I did a doctor role in *The Shootist* with Duke Wayne for old time's sake, and it didn't work. Westerns are too soft. You can't do psychology in spurs. I can't wait to get back into a real saddle. We've got to get back to real shoot-em-ups like John Ford used to do."

When conversation turns to the golden era of movies, he brightens. A soft blue horizon focuses in his clouded eyes. It's a subject he cherishes, for obvious reasons. He was one of the foundations. "We don't have any more men like Thalberg, Harry Cohn, Louis B. Mayer or the Warner brothers. These men were not only moguls—they also loved the picture business and had uncanny judgment about how to serve the public.

"I didn't know my movies like *Philadelphia Story* or *Ziegfeld Girl* or *Destry Rides Again* or *The Stratton Story* would become classics. I was too busy making three pictures at the same time. My generation was so busy we all took it for granted. The minute you finished one, you were off on another one that was gonna be better. I don't feel the same creative attitude on today's films. They're made too much by committees.

"They get a young guy with a pretty good track record now and when he finishes a picture, it gets turned over to another bunch of guys who four months ago were bankers in New York and they're passing judgment on some other guy's picture. There are too many strangers to the trade and hell, they don't even stay around long enough for anyone to get to know them. It's easy enough to sit around and bitch about the thing. You can call it sour grapes. But they call my time in movies the golden era. I'll accept that. It was. They say, 'Don't live in the past.' I quarrel with that. The invitations I get from college symposiums indicate that a whole new generation of respect is developing for old movies. It's not 'Give me the good old days,' because you ain't never gonna get the good old days back again. But it's not a bad idea to look back and learn from those days, to cull what was good from them. Eighty or ninety million people a week went to those movies. They say it's because they didn't have anything else to do, but I think there was more to it than that.

"Today you get porno, sex, violence—the pictures are all alike. It's a medium that has a tremendous capacity for showing all sorts of things, but we're not getting any variety. Films have become cynical, hopeless, worrisome. There are no new trends. Everything's been done already. There are no new Jimmy Stewarts because there are no vulnerable heroes in the world. Today's heroes are all seeking some kind of violent revenge against society. The bad guys have become good guys, and the good guys have become villains."

He started out at three hundred dollars a week at the insistence of his chums Margaret Sullavan and Henry Fonda, landed a seven-year contract, and learned on the job. Nobody in Hollywood has ever accused him of harboring any secret vice. In his cracker-barrel philosophy, sex is sacred and drugs are things you get prescriptions for. "I was too busy to get drunk or run around with broads. Then the war came and I was away for four years and when I came back I had to start all over. I was so in love with the magic of movies I didn't even get married till I was forty. After working all day, we'd all go out and Judy Garland would get up and sing for an hour. I just couldn't believe I was part of all this."

That homespun calico curiosity spilled onto the screen, where he played a number of American heroes with absorbing honesty. Men like Charles Lindbergh, Monty Stratton, Glenn Miller. "I worked out with Stratton for three months before we shot *The Stratton Story*, so I could pitch just like him. But I still can't play a note on the trombone. My music teacher quit because he said the sounds I made were so terrible he went home and yelled at his wife. So we plugged up the trombone and he taught me how to breathe and spit, and then he stood behind the curtain and played all the old Glenn Miller arrangements. Lindbergh was the hardest thing I ever had to do. I felt totally inadequate, but I wanted to keep Jimmy Stewart out of it."

He has also managed to keep a bevy of luscious leading ladies out of his life as well. "I love every one of them until quitting time," he says. But surely there were some duds in the batch. "Well," he drawls, after being prodded for some dishy quotes, "you can't fault girls like Grace Kelly or June Allyson. But when I was doing *Vertigo*, poor Kim Novak, bless her heart, said, 'Mr. Hitchcock, what is my character feeling in relation to her surroundings?' There was silence on the set and Hitch said, 'It's only a movie, for God's sakes.' She never asked another question."

That's it? The revelations don't get any more juicy than that? "Well, there was that Raquel Welch girl. She came onto the set of a western I did with Dean Martin and started asking a lotta questions about 'psychological motivation.' So Dean turned to me and said, 'What the hell is she talking about?' I said, 'I think she'll be fine, but let's loosen her up.' So Dean and I had her over for dinner and got her good and drunk. She was OK from then on."

At this point, wife Gloria saunters in—tall, elegant, cool as taffeta. "Is he really this perfect?" I ask. Gloria says a lot of people think Jimmy is boring, but what you see is what you get. Any faults? "I'm lazy," says Jimmy, yawning. "You are not," counters Gloria. No problems in thirty years of marriage? She thinks. After a long pause, she says, "No, after a day kissing June Allyson, he was always glad to get home at night."

If Jimmy Stewart ever dies, it won't be one of those violent, front-page things. He'll go the way he planned it—choking to death on humble pie.

21

CANDICE BERGEN

CANDICE BERGEN ISN'T CANDY ANYMORE. SHE LOUNGES ON A WHITE sofa draped in chocolate brown, her hair still fresh from herbal shampoo. The groceries, delivered hours ago, stand by the door of her duplex apartment, unopened. The telephone rings, unanswered. She's an angelic embroidery, illuminating radiance while the world waits and the rain falls on Central Park. Her eyes, like Tiffany rings, flicker with mischievous intelligence. She seems too good to be true. Or, as Shaw would have observed, too true to be good. She makes things work.

Born to luxury, the child of Hollywood celebrities, an acknowledged beauty since the age of diapers. An overnight star from the minute Sidney Lumet saw her modeling in a photo while still a student at the University of Pennsylvania and cast her in *The Group*. She's been trying it out, examining all the angles ever since. She writes alarmingly well. Her photography has been bought by magazines that count. Movie marquees light up with her name. It's never been enough. For years, she's been turning a profit by bringing visual aid to notoriously forgettable movies. Since she's done everything else, why not try being the first American star to appear in English in a film by Italy's tough, turbulent Lina Wertmuller? She did just that. It's called *The End of the World in Our Usual Bed in a Night Full of Rain* and it's awful. But the surprise is that Candice Bergen emerges from the wreckage a viable, visible, victorious new star. She is—are you sitting down?—the best thing in it. It's worth a visit, on a day full of rain, to talk to her about it.

"I took a chance," she says flatly. "It was a professional risk. I just can't make any more films for the wrong reasons, with polite, courteous directors who told me good morning and good evening and very little in between. Films where you spend your life chewing Juicy Fruit and throwing a Frisbee around and making phone calls and writing letters between takes. I really wanted to make a film where I was pushed, and I knew from the start what kind of film it was. I knew Lina would make demands and stretch me. She worked night and day forcing me to drop my defenses and wear through my protective armor and she did it with total force. It's the first time I've ever used so much energy or looked so honest on the screen."

It took engineering. Wertmuller even twisted her boyish frame into miraculous cleavage. "It's impossible to be more flat-chested than I am, but Lina decided to change everything from my eyebrows to the color of my hair to my bust. I wore a nightgown throughout most of the film and I was perfectly willing to struggle by like the doorframe I am, but Lina said I wasn't sexy enough. So she had a nightgown constructed that was the most intricate piece of architecture. I'd like to rent it for the rest of my life."

Bergen plays an American photographer with feminist pretensions married to a Communist Catholic journalist, played by Giancarlo Giannini. One of the problems is that she doesn't have a clearly defined role. Why, for example, can't a flat-chested woman also be sexy? "Don't ask me," she sighs. "Lina doesn't have the most womanly mentality. She doesn't think like the quintessential female. She's not American, she's not a feminist in any sense that we know. Italian feminism is archaic and outdated by ten years. It's really just budding there and it's more surrealistic than anything in this country. She also doesn't have a very accurate picture of the way Americans think. I knew from the beginning there would be problems. She said she'd be flexible about script changes, but we ended up in heated debates over every word. All I was able to do was Americanize my own dialogue as much as I could and try to modify and take out all of the political stuff that was irrelevant. Some of the original lines were things we were saying in America seven years ago and they just seemed ludicrous. The film was written in Italian and translated literally into English. The dubbed version works one hundred percent better."

When she arrived in Rome, Bergen couldn't even order a sandwich from room service. Three months later, with the aid of a Berlitz cassette and a book, she was speaking Italian so fluently she even spent an extra four weeks dubbing her own voice into the Italian version. "The film has more humor, color and integrity in Italian. But whether it gets creamed by critics or not, I learned more from it than ever before. I used to choose movies for the locations, because I'd never been to Hong Kong, or I wanted to go to Greece. Then I started choosing movies because the money was too tempting to turn down, so I did them for greed. My timing is too important to do that anymore. I will not leave my life for three or four months to do a movie unless it matters to me or will change me in some positive way. I only took this movie because I thought it represented a chance to grow. I've never been readier. I took the gamble, knowing all along it might not be the greatest movie ever made."

The most difficult thing about working for Wertmuller, she says, was not the "traumatic working conditions, although it was the most taxing film I've ever done physically. I didn't care about the exhaustion, because she gives off so much adrenaline that I didn't yawn for four months. I'm usually conked out in my trailer, eating and getting so groggy I can hardly go into the next scene. What was hard was that I never felt she liked me. Some directors break through your armor by hugging you and loving you. She never stopped assaulting me. The content of the film was the most depressing, despairing, despondent stuff. I spent four weeks crying every day, then two weeks in the rain with water pouring all over me, screaming all night. Every day was a psychodrama. But I can usually charm people, and if it's important, I can win them over. I never felt I could win her over. She and Giancarlo have a unique mother-son relationship that is complex and fascinating to watch, so I felt like the unloved child at times. But the worst part was that I kept wondering why she hired me. I was perversely opposite to what she wanted. She kept saying 'Be more Italian!' and I kept thinking, Well, why didn't she hire Silvana Mangano? It was hard feeling I never earned points and it was hard to resist the impulse to win approval."

Giannini, on the other hand, was "an angel, the perfect balance from Lina. He spent hours trying to explain Lina and talking to me about the film. He's an electronics wizard. He's a great comic. He's not very happy in life, but he makes everyone around him laugh." And still, it worked out in the end. "Lina taught me so much that I don't think I'll fall into the same behavioral traps I did before. I feel more open to work, more committed. I will no longer work for money. I'll write a book for the money or work for Cie perfume for the money. People say you can't stop making films. But I will. Or I'll go to class, but I won't make bad movies anymore. I'm far from being a vapid person, so why waste time looking vapid in vapid movies?"

She's smart enough to know the mistakes she made in her early films and says most of them "embarrass me so much I wish I could burn them and start all over. I paid for the kind of person I was then. Nineteen, saying 'I don't want to do movies' while doing movie after movie. I was a dilettante. And I feel guilty knowing serious, dedicated actors who would do anything for a small part in anything and I look back and see the big parts that were handed to me and the way I walked through them and was contemptuous of the work and I read the dumb interviews I did then and I would like to kill myself for all that, for all the growing up I did publicly and on the screen. I know actors who are brilliant and gifted, who know more about acting than I will ever know until I die, who have given me a respect for acting I never had in my life before. Then I see the chances I got and really abused and totally took advantage of my luck and never used it or learned from it—and it's very painful."

It's not her fault that there's no justice in the world about who gets the jobs, but she's uncannily wise to realize she "became a celebrity before I knew what to do with it. I did all of my trying out so publicly that I got crucified for all the mistakes I made because I was making them on film instead of in an acting class or on a little stage in summer stock. It was very hard standing there like an ass, saying and doing things that were dumb. So I used to go through movies winking or grinning to let the audience know I knew what they were watching was dumb. It was an apology, and it was unfair to me, to my co-workers, and to the audience. Now I'm resigned to getting creamed. I wouldn't know what to do if I didn't get creamed by some people. I did a terrible film called *The Domino Principle* because it gave me a chance to play an ordinary woman. I put on a sappy wig and wore sappy clothes and for once in my life I didn't look like Candice Bergen and they creamed me for that, saying I looked like Shelley Winters! If I take a risk, they kill me. If I don't, they kill me."

No matter. She knows who she is. She's writing a full-length autobiographical book about growing up. She's shelving her photography for the moment because she says it's "mediocre," concentrating on films and writing, and on a new romance that has "taught me a lot about love and belonging to somebody." And in the last analysis, she's got the last word. "If it comes down to being dumb and successful in movies or intelligent and successful in life, I think I'd rather be intelligent and successful in life."

Maybe Lina Wertmuller got more of a woman than she realized.

Jacqueline Bisset FROM THE AUTHOR'S COLLECTION

Lucille Ball LUCILLE BALL PRODUCTIONS, INC.

PHOTO © KORODY/SYGMA

Jimmy and Gloria Stewart

Candice Bergen

Walter Matthau

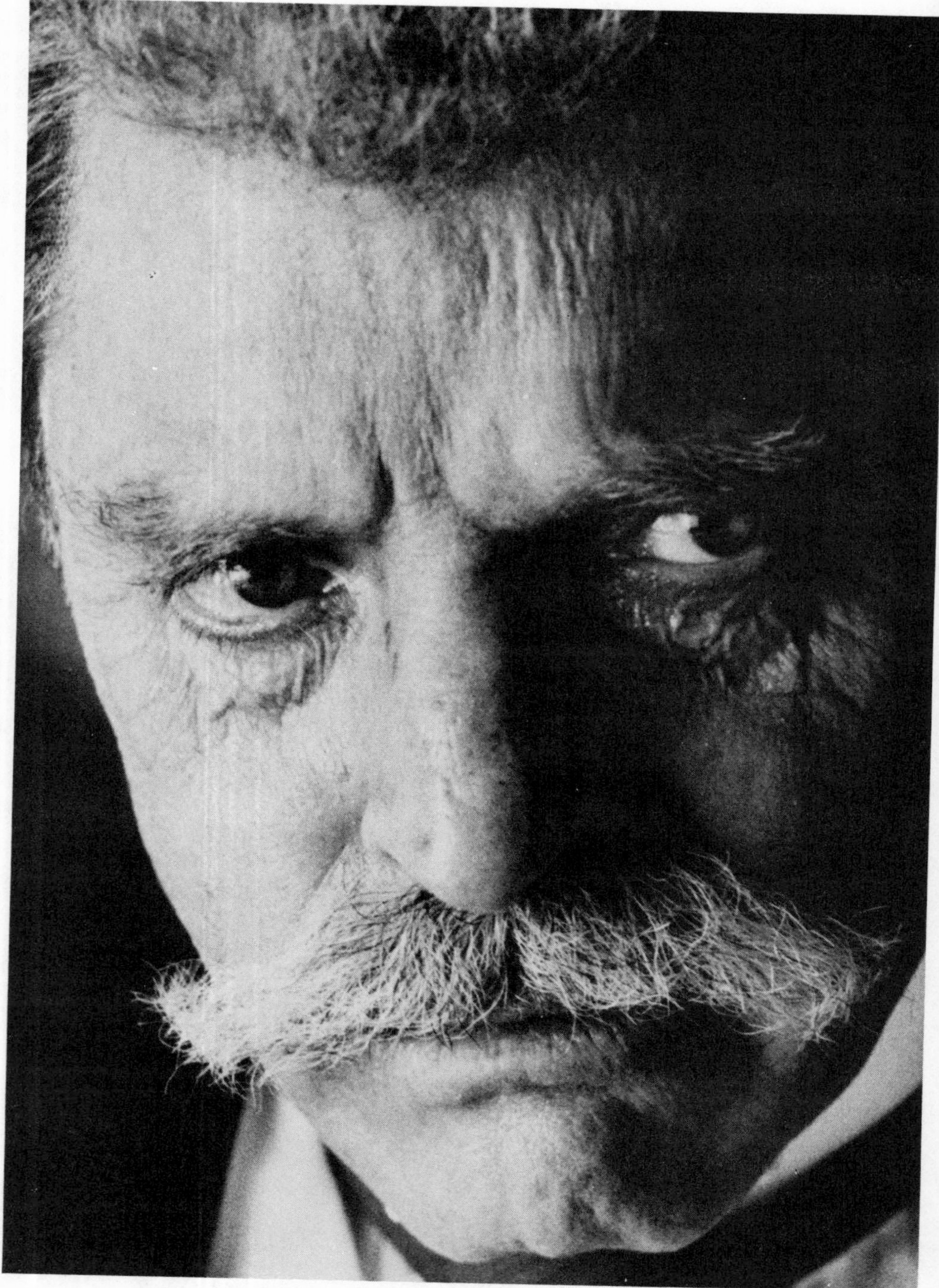

Burt Lancaster PARAMOUNT PICTURES CORP.

Bonita Granville and Lassie

FROM THE AUTHOR'S COLLECTION

Lauren Hutton

22

WALTER MATTHAU

PAUL NEWMAN HAS BLUE EYES. ROBERT REDFORD HAS MOLES. BURT Reynolds has muscles. Walter Matthau has none of the above, yet he gets just as big a salary, he works more often, and he's not twenty-five years old anymore. He's got the polltakers and soothsayers in Hollywood totally baffled. "I guess the reason I'm successful," he says, scratching his chin, "is because I'm interesting. I'm a good actor and I'm interesting. And I think people constantly want to know what I'm going to do. Or what I'm going to say. And I'm unpredictable, too, because I myself don't know what I'm going to do next. There's a bit of insanity running through my life."

And he then proceeds to demonstrate, in a conversation that careens like a roller coaster, but is never dull. His gambling orgies are legendary. In Ruidoso, New Mexico, where parts of his new film *Casey's Shadow* were filmed at the million-dollar All American Futurity race, he blew so much money at the track between scenes his wife, Carol (the former Mrs. William Saroyan), thought they'd have to hitchhike home to Beverly Hills. At a recent press junket to the

Santa Anita track to publicize the film, he blew another $3,500 between interviews. "I've lost a fortune. Betting to win is not my objective. My objective is simply to experience some kind of apprehension that spurts blood into my coronary arteries from my adrenal glands and constricts them. And as soon as my coronary arteries get constricted, I feel terrible, which is the kind of feeling I'm comfortable with. If I'm a loser, then I don't have to feel guilty about being a success."

"Does Carol try to keep you away from the track?"

"She's very sweet and generous about it. She knows it's a disease and she doesn't try to tamper with something she doesn't understand."

"Have you ever owned any horses yourself?"

"I was once asked to invest three thousand dollars in a half-interest in a horse and I said no, so the man who wanted to be my partner got so mad he said, 'OK, then I'll ask Telly Savalas,' and Telly Savalas did buy in and the horse, which cost six thousand dollars, has already won three hundred eighty thousand dollars and that's Telly's Pop. The same thing happens in *Casey's Shadow*. I play an old Cajun who gets a chance to enter a broken-down nag in the Futurity and I win the race."

"It's a family picture, isn't it?"

"I call all pictures that are good pictures 'family pictures.' If I like a picture I consider it a family picture. I'm very prejudiced."

"I don't remember you in any films with overt sexuality."

"How about *Candy*? But I don't think sex is necessary to a film. If you see a man fornicating with a goat, it's boring, mediocre. It doesn't really do anything for me. Whereas if I am allowed to use my imagination, I might think up all sorts of dramatic fantasies. Private bodily functions should not be shown on the screen. And I think lovemaking is a private moment, just like going to the bathroom."

"Do you ever ask to have things eliminated from a film?"

"Always. Always. I've asked many times. Writers just fall apart with the freedom of being able to use four-letter words. I generally suggest when I think they're not needed, to delete them. And it generally turns out for the best."

"Do you try to choose roles audiences will love?"

"I'm trying desperately to get out of that lovable, huggable good-guy image, but the banks put up the money and they like me in those parts. I've tried to do something different with each role. I think I fall into a category that doesn't have too much competition. It's the older leading man with a kind of sincere and roguish warmth. Which is not anything like my own personality."

"What's your own personality?"

"Mean, spiteful. Short-tempered. Suspicious. Jealous. Selfish. Ungiving. Et cetera."

"What kind of mail do you get?"

"They say, 'You're just wonderful and I'll bet you're such a swell guy and such a nice fellow and it's so great to know that you're going to see a Walter Matthau picture and know that there isn't going to be all that violence and sex.' But I don't shy away from violence and explicit sex if the part calls for it. Hell, I would do Macbeth stark naked if it was necessary. I think we'd have a little trouble with some of the Shakespeare soliloquies, like 'Is this a dagger, which I see before me . . .' "

". . . Or are you just glad to see me?" Laugh. "Isn't there always a thread of humor running through your work and your life?"

"I laugh a lot. My wife's very funny. My son, Charley, is very funny. I think I'm better at comedy than the other stuff. But I'm not a big laugher. I like Gene Wilder. Henny Youngman makes me laugh. He's one of the classic comics. But there's not much to laugh at."

"Did you laugh at all when you were doing *A New Leaf*?"

"Yes, I love Elaine May. Elaine May is so crazy and funny that I think she is totally insane. I once accused her of that and she got angry. She hates to be considered a cerebral humorist. Her father was a traveling Jewish comic who did all the tumbles and falls and pies in the face and shtick and Elaine insists that's what she does, too. Most directors are uptight and worried about budgets and deadlines, but not Elaine. She was marvelous. Of course, it's true that she went two million eight hundred thousand dollars over budget and therefore reduced the possibility of a profit to zero, but it was a lot of fun."

"Was working with Tatum O'Neal on *The Bad News Bears* at all funny?"

"Yeah, I liked Tatum. Tatum hollered '*Action!*' before the director did once. And I said wait a minute, I cannot act when an eleven-year-old child hollers action, I said to the director. Would you mind cutting? He said, 'Cut.' And I said, 'Tatum, don't do that. Don't holler action before the director. That is the director's job.' And she said 'OK' and went on chewing her gum. She just needed someone to tell her."

"So there was never any rivalry between the two stars?"

"Oh, my God, no. Tatum just wants to be treated like a little girl, which is what she is. Most people treat her like some kind of a freak, you know, who makes three hundred fifty thousand dollars a picture." Pause. "I guess that is a freak."

Despite his amiable personality, Matthau is like an Easter egg—hard-boiled on the outside, soft yolk on the inside. Many of his fellow actors have had problems cracking the shell. On *Hello Dolly!* he fought so much with Barbra Streisand it led her to utter one of her rare witticisms: "The name of this picture is not *Hello, Walter!*" From all reports, no love was lost between Matthau and Glenda Jackson on the current *House Calls*. He has so many neuroses there's no time left over to lavish compassion on other actors. One exception is his constant friend, co-star and fellow sufferer, Jack Lemmon. "I once leaned across a dinner table and asked Laurence Olivier if he had seen Jack Lemmon in *The Entertainer* and he said 'Oh, noooo!' and I said, 'Well, you should see it, because he's much better than you were in it.' Olivier went into shock. Then I said, 'You're much better playing kings, barons and dukes.' A few days later my housekeeper said Lord Olivier called. So I called him back and said, 'Lord Olivier, please,' and he said, 'Whoooo?' I said, 'Is this the lord?' And he was very cute. He said, 'No, this is the king, the baron, and the duke—who the hell are you?' Very cute, very cute."

Matthau's gambling is not his only sickness. He suffered a heart attack years ago, and just before *Casey's Shadow* he survived open-heart surgery for a blocked artery. During the recuperation period, one of the blood transfusions contained hepatitis virus, so he did all of the riding sequences in the film with hepatitis, resulting in damage to his liver enzymes. "I hyperventilate a lot, but it's no worse than waiting for the results on Oscar night. I jog a mile a day. Actually, it would be a good idea if they had all of the Oscar contenders jogging up and down the aisles. They could call it 'Jog for Oscars.' "

"Any long-range career plans, or have you done it all and now just want to do more of it?"

"You got it. I'm doing things in movies that I feel I've already done before. I was better onstage. In movies, I don't have much control and I don't really know what I'm doing. I just depend on the director and when things really get rough I just remember what Kim Novak told me: she said just speak softer and softer until they are forced to listen. It's true. When you're screaming on the screen people tend to want to run out and buy popcorn."

"Do you ever see yourself retiring?"

"Not unless I become physically disabled. I enjoy the whole bouillabaisse of making a movie—the whole stew pot, the crackling activity, the locations, the grips, the man who cleans the trailers, the screaming and yelling. Being a movie star is like being a general on maneuvers. I guess if I drop dead a lot of people are out of work."

"Are you going into directing?"

"I thought you were gonna say are you going to drop dead. Uh, no. I did direct a movie in 1958 called *Gangster Story*. It was a poor script by a hack writer and a famous cardiovascular surgeon who produced the film with his brother who was a textile manufacturer from Philadelphia. I made out the W-2 forms and held the boom and it was a terrible picture. You can still see it at four o'clock in the morning on TV."

"Who was in it?"

"My wife, Carol, who would be a great actress if she'd stop smoking."

"Have you stopped smoking?"

"Oh, yes. I had a heart attack eleven years ago and I was told that smoking closes your arteries, so I stopped. My only vices now are gambling. I play cards and I live at the track. I don't drink much and I don't smoke, but I get mean and I try to stop it but I can't."

"How do you relieve these tensions? Do you pour water on a cat?"

"I cry. After I get rotten, I just cry and when Carol sees me crying she goes crazy with grief. I went to a psychiatrist once and it depressed me so much I went straight to the race track and lost a thousand dollars and that cured me forever."

"Of gambling?"

"No, of the psychiatrist."

Now he just sticks Vicks VapoRub in his nose to breathe, chews three packs of sodium saccharine sugarless Carefree bubble gum a day mixed with chocolate syrup, and—luckily for us all—works it out at the movies.

23

SUSAN SARANDON

DEAD TULIPS LITTER THE FLOOR OF SUSAN SARANDON'S EMPTY white room on Beekman Place. "I haven't had time to clean them up and now I kind of like the look." She's sipping hot water with honey to soothe a case of laryngitis that makes her sound like the demon in *The Exorcist* and trying to talk about the sensation she's caused in *Pretty Baby,* the new Louis Malle film about life in the turn-of-the-century Storyville (New Orleans) red-light district, when columnist Earl Wilson calls.

She lies on the white floor and says, "Look, I don't know why you are so concerned about me taking off my clothes in front of an eleven-year-old child. Brooke Shields was posing nude long before I was." She covers the phone and makes a face, then talks into the phone again: "I play a prostitute in the film and Brooke Shields is my daughter, who becomes a child prostitute. What's wrong with that? Have you seen the picture?" She covers the phone again and whispers, "He hasn't even seen the picture." Then: "Look, Mr. Wilson, just say she goes to bed with her first customer the way most other kids go to their first prom. *Prom.* P-R-O-M . . ."

She hangs up, weary. The controversy nags her like the sore throat. "I don't know why everybody is making such a big deal out of this movie. I guess it's because of all the furor these days over kiddie porn. It's not at all sensational and I am absolutely flabbergasted over the fuss it's causing. There are no explicit sex scenes. It's a very disturbing theme for people, and because there's nothing prurient in it, they get even angrier.

"If Louis had shown Brooke having sex with that old man on camera, people would really be able to say, 'Look what they did to that kid!' But I think the film treats sex very coyly. I get out of bed naked, there's some nudity, but nobody tried to shield Brooke from anything. She turned twelve during the filming and she understood everything about the film, so there was nothing to shield her from. She's incredibly bright. She's not at all naïve, she's been on her own longer than I have. If you're making a movie about Storyville, you can't have people lying in bed with the sheets double-taped across their breasts the way they do in Doris Day movies."

Susan is now playing a gypsy in *The King of the Gypsies.* Brooke Shields is once again playing her daughter. Off-screen, Susan has left her husband, Chris Sarandon (who played Al Pacino's transsexual boyfriend in *Dog Day Afternoon*), and moved in with French director Louis Malle. If it all sounds confusing to you, consider the shock to Susan's family.

The oldest of nine children, she was raised a strict middle-class suburban Catholic from Edison, New Jersey. She was sent to convent schools before she graduated from Catholic University in Washington, where she met Sarandon and got into the Bohemian world of acting. "My parents have never discussed any of my movies with me, good or bad," she says. "My mother thinks I'm crazy and immoral, but my father, who used to be a band singer, told me the other day he plans to become a character actor when he's sixty-five. I'm sending him to my agent. One sister was my stand-in for two films, but she decided it was too much work, so she's having a baby this month, and I'll use the newborn baby for my baby in *The King of the Gypsies.*"

She says she was never a "flamboyant, antisocial rebel. I was just a hard-core misfit. I never went steady in high school, never fell in love, never had any close friends. I never planned a career. I went to Catholic University because I could live at home with my grandparents, who lived near the campus. I majored in military strategy. While I was there, I started modeling. The first modeling job I got was a selling folder for the Watergate building. Boy, that's a collector's item now."

She married actor Chris Sarandon in her junior year, followed him to New York after graduation, and accompanied him on an audition because he needed someone to read with him. Susan got signed. Without ever taking a single acting lesson in her life, she landed one week later in the film *Joe*, playing the teen-age daughter who got murdered by her own father.

The Sarandons moved into an empty apartment with one sofa next door to critic Clive Barnes. Soap operas, commercials and two movies later, she ended up in Hollywood. "I thought it was all a joke. I still didn't consider myself an actress, but I was making more money than my husband because I was in movies and he was in the theater. I never did get around to taking acting classes." She was the girl who fell off the wing of Robert Redford's plane in *The Great Waldo Pepper*, the fiancée of Jack Lemmon in *The Front Page*, and the Southern belle who drove F. Scott Fitzgerald wild in the highly acclaimed TV special "The Last of the Belles."

The pressures of sudden acclaim and growing up in public took their toll on her health and her marriage. "I lived in a Hansel-and-Gretel world of magic make-believe and while I was in London in the dead of winter making *The Rocky Horror Picture Show* I got pneumonia, my weight dropped to eighty-five pounds and I started hallucinating and finally had a severe nervous breakdown. I just dropped out of life and tried to figure out what I was doing with my life. I didn't work for a year and the marriage just fell apart."

After eight years of marriage, Susan and Chris separated about two years ago, but they're still best friends. "We grew up together; I've known him since I was seventeen. We still share the mortgage on a country house in Pound Ridge. It's been a great haven through all the trials and tribulations. When he's in town, he stays there. When he's away, I stay there. Or I sublet somebody else's apartment like I'm doing now. I have no home. We still have all of our money in the same bank account. We never really got around to separating anything. I rely on his taste and he reads all of my scripts and we give each other notes. Unfortunately, he's never offered anything but homosexual roles since *Dog Day Afternoon.* I've been luckier. They can't pigeonhole me."

With her floppy mane and her bulging, inquisitive eyes, she can play just about anything, although she's never sure what she's just done until she sees the final product. "I always look different in everything, which confuses people. I took *Pretty Baby* because I had never played a prostitute or a mother before.

"I'd much rather do character roles. Leading roles for women are very boring, but the supporting cast is always much more interesting. Sometimes you get caught up in the star thing and they talk you into things for your career. That's what happened with *The Other Side of Midnight*. Everyone said, 'C'mon, Susan, you've got to make a commercial movie.' Which was OK, except that it was a soap-opera melodrama and they treated it like it was Chekhov. I chewed a lot of gum while doing that one."

Then came Louis Malle and *Pretty Baby*. A fluke, she says. "He had never heard of me, but my name was on a list of actresses and Polly Platt, who was married to Peter Bogdanovich, liked me, and she wrote the script, so I had a ten-minute meeting with Louis and he said, 'There's nothing to be done until we find the little girl because there should be some resemblance between the mother and daughter.' So a month went by and I got a call asking if I could fly down to New Orleans to meet him. I couldn't go, so more time elapsed and then nobody liked the script for *Pretty Baby* and my friends all thought it was too small a part. Which it was.

"It was the little girl's picture. But I had just come from a big factory picture, a big industry film, and I thought working with a small group in a community effort would be a total change from *The Other Side of Midnight*.

"I had seen Louis' movie *Murmur of the Heart,* about child incest, and I thought it would be a challenge. Then a weird thing happened. Neither of us talked and they started negotiating a contract anyway. So finally he called me and I said, 'Do you understand what's going on?' Neither of us were participating, yet people were arranging our lives for us and I asked him if he believed in fate. We had this very strange conversation. And I said, 'I don't have any idea what I'm doing, in terms of this movie.' And he said, 'Well, neither does the character you're playing, so don't worry about it.'

"Then I found out he thought he was talking to Susan Blakely, not Susan Sarandon! He thought he was hiring Susan Blakely, another actress, who had also met him for ten minutes! I was totally confused. Then they made it worse by calling and Polly Platt asking me, 'You do have blue eyes, don't you?' and I said, 'You know very well I have brown eyes.' Then she said, 'There's this line about your nice breasts, well, how are your breasts? Do you have any breasts at all?'

"Well, by the time I got off the plane, you know, I was totally convinced they were going to take one look at me and throw up. I looked at Brooke Shields and thought, I don't look like Brooke at all, what am I doing in this film? And I just walked around New Orleans in the French Quarter in the one-hundred-degree heat and suddenly I said what the hell. It was one of those things."

So was her romance with the director. Now Susan shuttles back and forth from whatever rented home she's in to Louis Malle's apartment in Paris. She says she's crazy. Getting used to living in an adult world is as difficult for Susan Sarandon as giving articulate interviews. Reading through a two-hour transcript of an evening in her company has left me as confused as she is. Only one thing is certain: It's always nice to see a new star on the rise, and Susan Sarandon's star is rising so fast the noise is deafening. Trouble is, I can't stop worrying about those dead tulips.

24

BURT LANCASTER

As soon as you leave the manicured, cool green Beverly Hills of Los Angeles, the sun—which only moments ago was something to bathe in—becomes cruel and punishing. You start to sweat and your back sticks to the fake leather seat of your rented Monarch. Your eyes squint from the glare on the shadeless stretches of cement called civilization. That is, if you are headed for Century City and an ivory-colored stone tower where works one of Hollywood's most venerable living legends—Burt Lancaster.

Inside these newly acquired offices, Burt's charming young secretary offers instant coffee and excuses for her boss's tardiness. The place is a mess of not yet organized furniture and memorabilia. A fake Spanish dining room set fills one small room while a quixotic collection of antique leather settees, horn chairs, mirrors, books, and a huge glittery desk—all sized to make a giant comfortable—clutters another. To pass the time, I peruse a leather-bound volume of photos taken on the set of Bernardo Bertolucci's still-to-be-seen-by-Americans movie *1900.* The photos of the film, in which Burt stars as an aging, cruel Italian padrone, are breathtaking and make me long to see again the five-and-a-half-hour film I first viewed in 1976 at the Cannes Film Festival.

The door opens and, as if born on a charge of electric energy, in storms an enormous mass of hair, hide, thongs and fringe. Adidas or Pumas or some sort of jogging sneakers cover bare feet, sprung out of slightly short, navy-blue terry jogging pants. A handwoven shawl—something the Mexican Indians call a *quechquemitl*—covers the huge leonine shoulders. Over one is slung a well-worn, bruised leather pouch, bursting with papers, scripts and mail. A hat, equally battered and looking like a relic from the old Butterfield Express mail route, clings to the back of a tangle of silver hair which runs into a messy silver-and-red beard. Over all is a slightly salty dampness that makes everything about this wild-looking man curl.

Out of the hirsute nimbus flash familiar flinty blue eyes. There, too, are the massive white teeth clenched in the famous almost cynical smile so recognizable to moviegoers throughout the three decades Burt has reigned as one of those most wondrous and enigmatic of human animals—the movie star.

Thirty-one years ago, Burt Lancaster was an unknown actor appearing in *The Killers,* which made him famous overnight. A few weeks from now, Burt's sixty-first film, *The Island of Dr. Moreau,* based on H. G. Wells' science-fiction thriller, will open nationally. In it Burt stars as the genius whose genetic experiments lead him to turn animals into humans. It is a frightening subject which current society can worry about right along with the DNA controversy.

But at this moment, Lancaster hardly resembles a scientist. He looks more like one of the film's "humanimals," as the realistic little beasties are trademarked by their creators, John Chambers and Dan Striepeke, the same team who designed *Planet of the Apes.*

Unloading his hat and pouch, but retaining his shawl, Burt hurls himself behind his desk and offers me a seat on the other side. My chair is made of a leather sling suspended between three crossed bones. (I'm not sure they were bones, but if they were, the creature they belonged to was sure shortlegged.) I can tell as I lower myself down onto this precarious perch that my chin will be somewhere about eye level to the desk. Not the best position to conduct an interview with a meticulous star who has already interviewed me on the telephone, warning against the asking of personal questions. Fortunately, a few years of therapy allow me to reject this suggested seating arrangement and I haul up a chair that doesn't look like it was made by a cave dweller. Looking up, I catch a steely glint of amused acknowledgment at my decision to avoid this calculated con. Perversely and immediately, I know I like Burt Lancaster.

Lighting an unfiltered Camel, Burt, still glistening with perspiration from having jogged five miles to this interview, sets up the first of many paradoxes studding both his professional and personal life. "I know—I live in a land full of health nuts and still I smoke. But I run every day to offset the effect."

Lancaster's voice is that of a Viking king, with perfect diction naturally rooted in the hard *e*'s and *th*'s of East Harlem tenement youth. "I also love living in California, though I'm one of the few actors who live in a high-rise apartment. I have a house up the beach, but it's too far to drive. I come in every day and talk to writers and read scripts. If I do nothing else, I read and read and read. In a funny way, I work harder here than when I'm making a movie."

One wonders why this reputedly rich actor works at all. "I need the money! Though I own only one dress suit and some trousers, somehow it costs me three hundred thousand dollars a year to live. I must work," he says emphatically.

Last year while Burt was busy in the Virgin Islands filming *Dr. Moreau*, two Lancaster movies were being shown—films which New York critic Howard Kissell called "primordial." They were *Twilight's Last Gleaming* and *The Cassandra Crossing*. Balancing these with Bertolucci's controversial masterpiece *1900*, I comment that not only is Burt a talented actor but a talented businessman, capable of treating himself as a commodity as well as satisfying his thespian desires.

Lancaster laughs and the floor vibrates under our feet. "Bob Aldrich is a sweetheart and I love him. I've made four films with him, and I confess I was disappointed in *Last Gleaming*. I think there were somehow it costs me three hundred thousand dollars a year to live. I must work," he says emphatically.

"Now, *Crossing* is a different tickle—broad kitsch—right? I can only tell you that I worked for two weeks and got a lot of money. Not only did I not get to see Poland or the Cassandra bridge, but I never saw the movie. Though I worked with the director, writing scenes for Richard Harris and Sophia Loren. The script was bad.

The director would get mad, yell at everyone: 'Hell, Lancaster and I worked our asses off to write these lines for you. You don't like them? Well, I'll let you have the original ones then, see how you like that!' Ha, ha. Actually I enjoyed sitting with the marvelous Ingrid Thulin and talking for ten days straight. My best line in that movie was 'Listen, why don't you just take the dog for a walk? Hello? Yes. Yes. The train is approaching.' "

Lancaster chuckles again. I ask how it came about that he made *1900.* He sits back. "Ever since I saw *Last Tango in Paris* I had wanted to work with Bertolucci. He came to see me and we talked and talked. He was raising the money and there was no way to talk about what my salary might be. So finally I said, 'Look, I'll do it for you for nothing.' Sure, I did! I wasn't doing anything at the time and it was only two weeks' work. So I went to Palma, Italy—right near where Bertolucci was born—and treated the whole thing like it was a vacation. I found the aging character I play a very rich, exciting part.

"When I was recently in New York I saw a screening Bob Evans gave at Paramount. There were two young men in the audience who were obviously—young—ha, ha—hippies, with long hair and crazy hats, blue jeans, T-shirts." (Burt is talking as if he hasn't looked in the mirror lately.) "Their names escape me, but apparently they own a record company and are very rich. They told me *Novecento*, which is the film's real name, would be released as soon as they had taken over the distribution rights. But I've never heard another word.

"It's more complicated than just the length of the movie. The reason is that Bertolucci contracted for a three-and-a-half-hour movie. He got something like six million dollars from three major film companies, Paramount, Twentieth and UA, each with their own distribution areas. I don't think Bertolucci had any intention of making a shorter film, however. The script I saw, which was only the first half, concerned only me and the old peasant, Sterling Hayden. It was one hundred eighty pages long. Our two sons, Robert de Niro and Gérard Dépardieu, were still little boys when it ended, so I knew there was going to be another whole movie there. As Carol Reed might have said, 'It was all very naughty.'

"The studios may not be able to force Bertolucci to cut, since they put the money up and refuse to show the film this way—one reason being that the left-wing political emphasis is so strong. This is the film's whole development and difficult to cut around. They feel U. S. audiences aren't interested in Italy's political problems. The studios were only looking for another *Last Tango*. Instead, Bertolucci has the old Red Square atmosphere on the march—though the sex scenes are more than explicit."

The sex in *1900* is certainly explicit, but never pornographic. Since many Italo-Americans wonder what happened back home in the old country, the studios could be guessing wrong. U. S. audiences might look to such a film to answer the nagging question of why there is so much Euro-communism today. And everybody would get to see both Burt Lancaster and Sterling Hayden's up-to-now-hidden sex appeal in the nude. Compared to what the film shows of De Niro and Dépardieu, the two old-timers are merely flashers. (But seriously, I think the industry should pull itself together and let audiences judge whether or not *1900* is too sexy, too political or too long.)

Burt sits puffing his endless Camels, reflecting. "It doesn't matter that Bertolucci was naugthy, he went ahead and made a marvelous movie: his creation. I remember being with Luchino Visconti on *Conversation Piece* when he stopped all shooting because he saw three TV antennae in the distance. I was getting fifty thousand dollars a week overtime and said maybe he should take some of my money back. He didn't approve of that. 'I stop shooting so my producers and crew learn I'm serious when I say no antennae. At times like this you must be intransigent.' " Again comes Burt's hearty laugh, dwindling to a chuckle of affection as he remembers the late, great maestro with whom he made a great film, *The Leopard*, and shared the same birthday, November 2.

"These men—Fellini, Visconti, Bertolucci, Antonioni—are extraordinary human beings. We have a whole thing in our system where people direct only for the sake of saying they are directors. Where is their background for directing—their education, intellectuality, imagination? You think of Ingmar Bergman. These are informed, erudite, knowledgeable, creative people. But because ours is a business of mediocrity, nine out of ten directors are only average craftsmen, but not imaginative.

"They are also part of a system where how much money the picture makes is the criterion for goodness. The pressure is so strong, they immediately attack a film on whether or not it's viable—a moneymaker. Think of the ego of Fellini when he says he is going to make a film costing *x* millions called *8½* because 'this is my eighth-and-a-half film and I have nothing else to say.' We don't make movies like that because we don't have men with egos like that—oh, we have egos in Hollywood but no one would want to make a movie about them.

"Fellini is like a great novelist or composer. Visconti was one of the greatest opera directors the world has known. He made Callas. I love opera. I once appeared on a TV show with Tony Randall and before the show I was telling him some of my own experiences and he said, 'Boy, you really know opera.' I said, 'Not as much as you. After all, you're on the board of the Metropolitan.' He said, 'Oh, I don't know anything; they tell me the answers.' Ha! You see—America, the beautiful. And the English—they butchered a respectable TV film I made, 'Moses.' They cut it for release in theaters so they could have a 'turnover.' It was dreadful.

"No, I'm not afraid of playing aging heroic characters. Hell, I'm sixty-three years of age. And I don't think Dr. Moreau is a heroic character. What we tried to do was play him as—what can I say?—obviously an unusual man, a man involved in his career, a strange man. So we played him dead straight on.

"We had moments that we put into the script like when the boy, Michael York, washes up onto the island half-dead. He's running through the jungle. He sees strange things—a cloven hoof, just shadows of a face like an animal. He is thinking he is mad. He falls in this animal trap. Well, 'they' were worried that this opening was too slow. They wanted a *Jaws* opening. I blew my top.

"Now, not with AIP or anyone else do I ask for final cut but I was worried about this opening scene. And there my contract protects me from any producer changing the whole concept of the script. It is important the movie reveal slowly the boy's mind. They wanted another man to be in the boat with Michael—almost dead. As Michael goes into the jungle, an animal hand would pull the man into the bush and then you'd see this bloody stump—the man being eaten.

"Well, if they use that kind of bloody opening, I can use my right to injunct them if I wish. I haven't seen the film yet, but I hear it's mighty entertaining—which is what we started out to make in the first place."

Burt Lancaster stopped talking and looked out the window as if his blue eyes could see across the Pacific. Here is a man with no new cinematic *1900*'s up his sleeve. He says, "Kirk Douglas and I are working on a project, but I am off to Australia and Bali. Why? Oh, just because I've never been there. I've only been as far west as Fiji. To you that's east? Well, that's what makes life interesting."

25

BONITA GRANVILLE & LASSIE

LASSIE, THE WORLD'S MOST BELOVED DOG, IS BACK ON THE SCREEN, and Bonita Granville, best remembered as the world's most contemptuous child, has put him there. To get the full story, you have to turn the clock back thirty-five years. In 1943, Lassie fell into the arms of a raven-haired child named Elizabeth Taylor in MGM's *Lassie Come Home* and the dog world was never quite the same again. That same year, a blond teen-ager named Bonita Granville was making a different kind of impact, getting flogged with whips by Nazi storm troopers in a shocker called *Hitler's Children*. The two stars were as far apart in style and quality as bones and Gainesburgers.

But this is Hollywood, where man's best friend is his box-office gross, and Lassie and Bonita are calling bygones what they are. For the first time in twenty-six years, Lassie is back, starring in a Grated musical called *The Magic of Lassie* (opening, ironically, at the Radio City Music Hall, where the first Lassie movie opened thirty-five years ago) and Bonita Granville spent two-and-a-half million dollars of her own money to get him there in Technicolor and Dolby sound. What's more, she's made Lassie bark for publicity. The things they've had this dog doing for newspaper space would make Rin Tin Tin turn over in his grave. Lassie, always the trouper, climbed to the top of the Empire State Building to get a "dog's eye view" of Gotham. Then Lassie danced with the Rockettes, performed during the Mets' doubleheader at Shea Stadium, and taught Ilie Nastase how to play tennis at Forest Hills. Lassie was even scheduled for a mayor's conference at City Hall before Mayor Ed Koch vetoed the whole thing. Smart move. New York has gone to the dogs enough already.

But wait. Before you call up the A.S.P.C.A., let Bonita Granville tell it. "Lassie, for all the breeding and training, is not at all neurotic. Rudd Weatherwax, who still owns Lassie, has always looked for a calm dog in each litter of pups to train for films. He never uses a chain for a leash and he never hits the dog. There have been seven generations of Lassies and they have all been males, so please don't write that Lassie has been a female impersonator for thirty-five years because it's been used before. The present Lassie is a direct descendant of the same Lassie who appeared with Roddy McDowall and Elizabeth Taylor in the first Lassie movie. He weighs eighty pounds, is two-and-a-half years old, and eats a pound and a half of meat a day plus training treats of cheese and liver tidbits. He stays in the best hotels and travels with a companion, who is an Australian silky. There have been six other Lassies, and I remember every one of them. The reason Lassie has always been male is because like all animal species, male collies are more beautiful than females. Female coats of hair shed too fast to get a matching shot on film. Also, they have more nervous problems. This Lassie is a total pro. On the first day, an arc light fell and the set caught fire. Lassie was so shaken he bolted over the bleachers and tried to jump out of a window. I thought we'd have to close down the picture. But he recovered."

Bonita (her friends call her Bunny) Granville was the meanest brat in movies during the late Thirties and early Forties. She had appeared in fifty-five films by the time she retired in 1947 to marry Texas oil millionaire Jack Wrather. Her father was a Broadway actor named Bernard Granville, who starred in the *Ziegfeld Follies.* At the tender age of seven, Bonita left Douglaston, Long Island, and moved to Hollywood, where Daddy had been hired by Warner Brothers to appear in three of that studio's first musicals. In the same apartment building where the Granvilles lived, a casting director spotted the blond moppet and asked her if she'd like to work with a new actor—"a Mr. Olivier from England"—in a film called *Westward Passage*. "Mr. Olivier from England" turned out to be Laurence Olivier and Bonita made her debut with him. The year was 1932. Four years later, she was nominated for an Oscar for destroying the lives of Merle Oberon and Miriam Hopkins in William Wyler's first film version of Lillian Hellman's *The Children's Hour,* called *These Three*. "I didn't know what a lesbian was," recalls Bonita, "but I knew the Ten Commandments and I knew what adultery was. They told me it was a movie about adultery."

In the intervening years, she denounced Claudette Colbert as a witch in *Maid of Salem*, tortured Bette Davis into a mental breakdown in *Now Voyager*, turned any number of stars in to the Nazis at MGM, and made life generally unbearable for Robert Taylor, Norma Shearer, Ann Sheridan, Jane Powell, Margaret Sullavan and countless others. Today, at fifty-five, Bonita looks back on those years with humor. "I played some horrible brats, but I also played a child dying of consumption in a John Ford film with Barbara Stanwyck. Nobody remembers that one. They only remember the brats." She was also the star of a series based on the Nancy Drew mysteries, and played Mickey Rooney's girl in some of the Andy Hardy films. Nobody remembers those, either, but the British Film Institute recently honored her with a five-day retrospective at the National Film Theatre in London. "I kind of set the record straight." She grins.

She met Jack Wrather on a blind date in 1947. He had just returned from the Marines and wanted to finance three movies with his oil money. Her publicist introduced them. "In one of the last films, I played a gun moll with a cigarette hanging out of my mouth who shoots Barry Sullivan in the end. My family sees these things on TV now and howls!" She gave up acting without a second thought, she says, "because Jack was not the kind of man who would put up with a wife who got up at five A.M. and came home at seven P.M." Also, she didn't need the money. Wrather owned Muzak and radio station WNEW in New York. Then, in 1956, the Wrathers bought the rights to Lassie and Bonita became the producer of the Lassie

TV series for most of its nineteen years on the air. "After nine years of the last series, we ran out of ideas. Now we've got some new ones. I've just done a two-hour pilot for a new Lassie series and I spent two years making *The Magic of Lassie* for theaters. We also own the Lone Ranger show, which is still in syndication. And you should see the revenue that comes in from merchandising."

No question about it. Lassie is rolling in diamond flea collars. In 1943, this canine superstar made $200 a week at MGM. Lassie No. 7 makes $150,000 a picture. And with advertising concessions, he's worth $300,000 a year to his trainer, and even more to the Wrathers, who are busily pushing Lassie flea collars, Recipe dog food with Lassie's photo on the cover of every can, plus Lassie T-shirts, leashes, combs, brushes and assorted "pet accessories." "We guard the properties very carefully," says Bonita. And while Lassie sleeps in his custom-designed kennel, the Wrathers supervise the two hotels they own at Disneyland. "Walt Disney asked Jack to build the first one, then I decorated all fourteen hundred rooms myself. That way, I can still be with Jack and keep myself busy at the same time."

Success hasn't turned her head. She still has old-fashioned values, and many people consider her slightly square in a town that is measured by the number of martinis you wolf down before lunch. "I do not believe Lassie movies are dated. What is becoming dated in my opinion is the endless repetition of sex and violence on movie and TV screens. I believe in good, clean, honest, family entertainment. The only way we can get people back into the movies is to make films for middle Americans who don't want to see and hear filth and four-letter words. I know all the four-letter words, but I don't use them. Films should be uplifting. Why show how awful the world is when we already know it? Lassie has been off the screen for four years now and my husband and I have been deluged with letters from Lassie's fans, wanting to know when their favorite dog would return. Lassie is a symbol of everything that is best in life—compassion, loyalty, faithfulness and decency. Kids come out of *The Magic of Lassie* with tears of joy streaming down their faces. I showed it to a very hard group of professionals and Hal Wallis and Mervyn Le Roy were crying, too. There's nothing corny about that kind of sentiment."

And to make sure the message meets the heartstrings, she's assembled a cast of clean-living nostalgia groupies for *The Magic of Lassie* that includes Jimmy Stewart, Mickey Rooney and Alice Faye. "I have always been in complete awe of movie stars," she says. "Frankly, I've admired Jimmy all my life—even though I know him socially and we go to the same parties. At sixty-nine, he's as popular as he ever was. He plays a grandfather who owns a small winery from which Lassie escapes. It's his seventy-sixth movie, and he even gets to sing one of the songs. Mickey Rooney, at fifty-seven, worked with me thirty-four years ago in *Andy Hardy's Blonde Trouble*. He plays the manager of a broken-down wrestler who rescues Lassie in the desert and takes him to a wrestling match. Alice Faye plays a singing waitress in a Reno café who befriends Lassie on his travels. Alice sings on film for the first time since 1962. And there are even songs by Pat and Debby Boone."

It sounds like an overdose of Binaca to me. But at a time when most Forties stars are either joining Alcoholics Anonymous or retiring to rest homes, Bonita Granville and Lassie are helping each other make spectacular comebacks. For the little girl who made a career in sadomasochistic psychodramas but "was never alone with a boy in a car until I was seventeen years old," Bonita must be doing something right. As for Lassie, make no bones about it. Life is a freshly painted fire hydrant.

Doggone right.

26

GERALDINE PAGE

GERALDINE PAGE HAS BEEN SITTING IN THE FLY-SPECKED BACKROOM of a mangy bar on rain-soaked Ninth Avenue for fifteen minutes while the photographer who has come to take her picture for this interview sips his beer nearby. "She's not here," he says glumly, when I arrive. Neither of us recognize one of the two or three greatest actresses in the American theater. Finally, the weathered lady who looks like somebody's housekeeper waves shyly. She isn't wearing one trace of makeup. Something resembling a wrinkled beautician's smock, with a beat-up raincoat around her shoulders, is what she's wearing. Her hair falls in wisps from an improvised braid wrapped around her head and she nurses a cup of stale coffee she won't drink until it's cold with an oily film circling the top, because that's the way she likes it.

She doesn't do many interviews ("They're usually actively destructive") and never under any circumstances is anyone allowed into her home—a rickety brownstone in Chelsea that says "TORN PAGE" on the door. It isn't clear why, since she cheerfully describes the interior as a place *House and Garden* might recommend for slum renewal. "The walls are covered with Crayola and watercolor drawings by the children and every time the painters come we ask them to paint around everything. There's so much rubbish piled all over the floor you have to step over it to get into the kitchen." If you want to reach either Geraldine or husband Rip Torn, you have to phone their agent, leave a message, and they call you back. They do their own scrubbing, occasionally take movie jobs to pay their mortgage, and Geraldine has supermarket boxes filled with unanswered fan letters piled all over the house that she never has time to open. Once she hired a secretary who corrected all of her grammar and spelling and it embarrassed Gerry so much she thanked the lady and threw all of the perfectly typed letters into the garbage can. Between jobs, the Torns lug dirt up five flights of stairs and plant apple, peach, plum and almond trees on their roof. They grow their own tomatoes, lettuce, zucchini and herbs, and their cornstalks are high as an elephant's eye. And they still have time to play Strindberg.

If this makes Gerry sound eccentric, she'd be the first to admit it. Except on her, it's charming. She's one of the most unpretentious stars ever encountered in the galaxy of greatness, and when you meet her you can scarcely believe she's the same dynamic talent whose name sends electric shocks through the hearts of aspiring actors everywhere who want to be just like her. Tell her she's great and she blushes, then shrugs. "Yeah, to you, me and my family, but nobody else!" Tell her she was beautiful once in Richard Brooks's film version of her stage smash *Sweet Bird of Youth* and she says, "When I saw myself on the screen, I wanted to drown myself!" She remains a total enigma to the employers, critics and fans who adore her, but when she works she busts out of her shopping-bag-lady persona and lightning strikes. She's currently on view in two new vehicles: *Nasty Habits*, a movie satire about Watergate set in a nunnery, which the Catholic Church has condemned, and "Something for Joey," a heartbreaking TV special April 6 on CBS. She doesn't talk about them much, except to say, "I'm Catholic in both—in the movie, I'm this ridiculous criminal nun modeled after Haldeman, and in the TV show, I'm a wonderful, devoted Catholic mother whose son is dying of leukemia. So if the Catholics get mad at me in the first one, they'll surely like me in the second." Geraldine was raised Methodist but it's obvious that life is her church and each day brings a new hymn.

She could have made millions, but says she and Rip are "poor but happy. We're not clever at business, agents, managers, or investing money wisely. And we've been ripped off outrageously. I turn down work constantly because I don't like to do things I think are really rotten. Sometimes they turn out to be smash hits, but I turn them down on a philosophical basis. I don't regret that. I turned down the mother in *The Exorcist* and that confused everybody because I turned up in *The Beguiled* chopping off Clint Eastwood's legs with an ax. But I really liked that character in *The Beguiled.* I also turned down the original starring role in *Who's Afraid of Virginia Woolf* and everybody thought I was crazy. I hate that play. I think its big success at the time was because people were shocked by so many four-letter words. Edward Albee is a wonderful plagiarist. He has wonderful taste in the people he steals from, mainly Strindberg. It turned out to be a big hit for Uta Hagen, who was my teacher for seven years, so I was very happy for her. I'd like to play a part like that, but in a better play."

She's always been a rebel. After *Summer and Smoke* catapulted her to stardom at the Off Broadway Circle in the Square, she turned down all spinster roles and accepted a seven-year contract in Hollywood, only to find herself bewilderingly co-starring with John Wayne in a 3-D western called *Hondo,* which she liked because "it was nice to the Indians." Wayne liked her so much he bought up half of her contract so she could do every other film with him. One day his driver picked up Gerry to drive to the set and stopped on the way to mail a package at the post office. "That's Duke's Christmas present to Senator McCarthy," he said. Her mouth flies open when she retells the story. "Knowing he was a charming, reactionary old guy who was doing a lot of right-wing propaganda movies, I said, 'Fine about the contract, as long as I have script approval.' That was my first mistake. The second mistake was when I was sitting around in the Mexican desert, waiting for them to fix the 3-D camera that was always breaking down, with Ward Bond, Mia Farrow's father and some of John Wayne's other cronies, who were all big McCarthy supporters, and Ward Bond said, 'I told that Pat girl not to go back to New York to do some goddam commie play by some goddam commie writer,' and I knew he was talking about Patricia Neal, who had left her contract to do Lillian Hellman's play *Another Part of the Forest*, and I said, 'I don't blame her—it's a great part!' Well. That did it. They all said,

'Oh, yeah—you studied with that Yewta Hay-gen, didn't you?' That was the end of my Hollywood contract. It was ten years later before I made another movie."

Gerry says she became politically aware about the time she met Rip Torn in *Sweet Bird of Youth*. He played Richard III as Richard Nixon, back in 1968, before Watergate, and she and Maureen Stapleton picketed Woolworth when blacks couldn't sit at lunch counters. Gerry announced to the press at the time: "Lorraine Hansberry and I went to the same Chicago high school and it didn't hurt either one of us." The Torns have been together eighteen years but "can't remember the wedding date." They have a daughter, Angelica, thirteen, and twin sons, Tony and John, eleven. Before Rip, she says, her whole life was acting. Now, it's less important. "I've worked in a thread factory, a negligee factory and a dime store. If you're a good actor, you should absorb everything. Acting led me into politics, sewing, skiing, skating, psychology, global affairs—everything that affects human beings. Rip once learned to play a Chopin nocturne for a role. Then he got mad because people said, 'You faked that beautifully!' The hardest thing I ever had to learn is how to belch on cue."

The suggestion she might be sublimating her own career for Rip brings a squeal of laughter. "On the contrary, the greatest roles I've done Rip has made possible. He's the one who got the Actors Studio Theater started with *Strange Interlude*. Rip got the rights to the O'Neill play, talked Jason Robards into it, talked José Quintero into directing it, and Lee Strasberg was so terrified he went to bed for three weeks with a sudden cold." A great controversy thundered when Rip and Gerry walked out of their beloved Actors Studio a few years ago and severed all relations with their mentor, Lee Strasberg. Resentment and anger still burns deep. According to Gerry, it all started when the London Festival asked the Actors Studio to take its productions of James Baldwin's *Blues for Mr. Charlie* and Chekhov's *Three Sisters* to England. She was pregnant with the twins and had to drop out of the Chekhov, but Rip was starring in the other play and producing it in an unofficial capacity. He tried to encourage Strasberg and director Burgess Meredith to speed up rehearsals and even gave Baldwin his personal promise that his salty dialogue would not be censored by the Lord Chamberlain. His efforts were rejected, he was fired, and Gerry said, "That's the end of the Actors Studio Theater." They lost two of their most prestigious stars, the company went unprepared to London, had a giant fiasco, and the Actors Studio never did another production. "We left and never went back. Rip never holds grudges, but I'm the one who is still bitter. Strasberg is a marvelous teacher, but you can't try to build a theater for him because he'll tear it down."

Considering the number of "method" actors (Monty Clift, Kim Stanley, Marilyn Monroe, James Dean, ad infinitum) who have ended up trashing their talent, how has she stayed so sane? "By playing characters that aren't me. I use acting to escape from myself, not to be myself. What I like most is violent contrasts. If I play a low-down, wicked drunk, I like to play a saintly, good, generous, modest person next. I had a wonderful time in *Absurd Person Singular* on Broadway. I was in it for two years, after everybody else left. But I want to do good stuff, too. That's why Rip and I are doing a repertory of Strindberg plays next. You can't pay the mortgage and buy a limousine doing Strindberg, so I'll end up doing another movie like *Pete and Tillie* with Carol Burnett. But I won't be repeating myself. Every role I've been offered since *Absurd Person Singular* has been another drunk. If I played another drunk now I'd have to water it down or figure out what's left in my drunk repertoire. I waited all this time between *Sweet Bird of Youth* and *Absurd Person Singular* before I could play another drunk with fresh enthusiasm."

Tennessee Williams, who always called her one of his three favorite actresses, hasn't come up with anything either. "He's not writing with his old power. All of his recent stuff is influenced by idiots who try to get him to be avant-garde. I'm just marking time till he gets through this phase. He's always saying he's dying, but he'll bury everyone first." So she grows zucchini, and waits. And one thing she's learned: You can't win 'em all. "Some critic came to see me in one of the Strindberg plays called *The Stronger*, she says, on the way back to her house from the bar, "and he wrote that I should watch my annoying vocal mannerisms. That made me furious." Why? Because she doesn't like bad reviews? "No," she roars, hilariously. "Because in that play I never speak one word of dialogue!"

They call her a kook, but the little girl who cried her eyes out as a child when her mother punished her for going swimming with her wrist watch on by forbidding her to see Bette Davis in *Now Voyager* is now having the last laugh. All the way to the poorhouse.

27

LAUREN HUTTON

CLICK! SHUTTERS SNAP, CAMERAS TURN, THE WHEELS IN LAUREN Hutton's head record it all, missing nothing. She's living a movie and trying to live her life at the same time. She's today, grabbing it all. Always moving. It's Persia and Indonesia today for *Vogue*, a mud ditch in Canada tomorrow for Robert Altman, headlines next week for saying that old forbidden four-letter no-no starting with *f* on Boston television. When does she rest?

She arrives for tea in blue jeans, a cotton shirt right out of Tom Sawyer, and a fisherman's hat—a curious, mysterious mixture of Huck Finn and Scarlett O'Hara. The public still thinks of her as the gap-toothed Revlon cover girl who is trying to get into the movies. Critically, she hasn't been taken seriously yet. "I didn't take it seriously myself. I'm just now beginning to see progress in my work and I'm just grateful whenever the critics don't punch me out," she says in that husky, melodious Southern drawl that digs its root canal straight down to the swamps of Florida, where she shot up like a grasshopper, never dreaming she'd someday grace every coffee table from here to Zanzibar and star in movies like *Welcome to L.A.* and the forthcoming *Viva Knievel* (with Gene Kelly as a seedy, alcoholic mechanic and Evel Knievel as himself). Not bad for a kid who never wanted to be anything more than Sheena, Queen of the Jungle.

Named after her father, Laurence Hutton, a disillusioned writer from Oxford, Mississippi, who grew up next door to William Faulkner, Lauren was born in Charleston, South Carolina, but moved to the swamps of Florida when her mother remarried, and spent her childhood fishing for alligators with cane poles, making rafts, collecting snakes and defying anyone to call her a Southern belle. To this day, she prefers lizards to limousines, and at various periods of her New York bachelor-girl life has lived with skunks, African chameleons and snakes ("but Manhattan is lousy for snakes," she adds, "—can't stand the steam heat!"). A continual school dropout, she's been on her own since the age of eighteen, when she fled to New Orleans and worked as a barmaid in Al Hirt's jazz club on Bourbon Street. "I was really tough. In the photos of me then I look older and meaner than I am now. I wore a short skirt and got pinched a lot, but I made five hundred dollars a week in tips. I rode back and forth from school on a motorcycle, went to class from nine to three and worked as a cocktail waitress from seven to four A.M. I saw some sick things, man. And I grew up fast. I also went through all my money because I hung out in the clubs all night. I was so tired I lost interest in everything, so I dropped out of college and all I wanted to do was go to Africa. So I came to New York with two hundred dollars in my pocket to get a tramp steamer bound for Africa and I had to get a job to pay for the trip. I became a model through *The New York Times.* I found a want ad for Christian Dior and worked five days a week from nine to six for fifty dollars a week and that's how I got started. It lasted ten years, till I got the Revlon contract."

She did not, she hoots with throaty laughter, sleep with the late Charles Revson to get the job. "Big romance? Are you kidding? *A*) I had my own romance going. *B*) I don't gap three generations just to get a job. I never even had a date with the guy." Nor did she attend his funeral. In real life, she doesn't even wear lipstick, a fashion secret that sends the Revlon execs scurrying to their shrinks for extra Valiums. Yet the image pays off no matter how you slice it. Four years ago, when Revlon offered her an exclusive contract for so much money she is forbidden to reveal the full details even now, Ultima II had been in the red for fifteen years. During the first year of her contract, sales shot up 60 percent. All of which leads one to believe a lot of female consumers want to look like Lauren Hutton.

"Don't you feel a responsibility to these faceless media-influenced masses?" I ask.

"Gee, I dunno. I don't think I've ever been asked that before. I'm not much to emulate. I've got one eye that crosses and there's that gap between my teeth. But that's how a lot of people recognize me—they look at me real close and then when I open my mouth I'm busted. It all came about because the dentist told my mother to leave my teeth alone because they'd eventually grow together. They never did."

So how does anyone get to be a famous model with a split between her teeth big enough to drive a small truck through? "Well, they lie for one thing. They say they're gonna get it fixed. And then they work very hard so that by the time the agency is about to drop them because they didn't, they're already bringing in a lot of money so they can't get fired." She means it. For some girls modeling would be enough if they got the fame and money ("You bet your ass!") Lauren got. But it wasn't enough "because I learned everything I could learn in the first three years. All I did was pose for pictures, then my old man and I would take six months off and spend all the money on travel."

Her "old man" is the same fellow who has been in her life for years, a young stock investor named Bob Williamson. She refuses to discuss him because "he's not a public person so he doesn't want publicity. He's a dynamite astronomer. The real star of us is him, so he doesn't need any fame. He likes me to be independent and take care of myself, but he also wants to live together, so we're finding a way of working that out. We're in a hot spot. He says all I need to do is relax and I'll be fine."

With that guaranteed income from Revlon, she doesn't have to do anything but brush her teeth and smile. But this is a driven girl—moving, searching, hanging out, studying people, cramming on a course called life and never quite sure whether or not she's flunked the exam. When she started acting, she was just another pretty face saying lines. She's getting better and it shows. "I was frightened in my first films, so I did what I knew I could do—pose and model my way through. I was just bluffing." Her first job, in a forgotten trifle called *Paper Lion*, came about "on a coffee table. There I was, on the cover of *Vogue*, and they had tested a lot of girls and the producer's wife looked down and said 'What about her?' I had been on a few interviews with producers who were typical lecherous Hollywood cigar-chomping clichés. But this time Alan Alda was in the office and they asked me to talk to him about football. So we tossed the ball around. Three days later, I was in Florida ready to shoot. I was absolutely terrified, not only because I was insecure but I had always been scared to death of football players and there I was, the only woman in a movie surrounded by massive guys in spring training. The first day Alex Karras hit me in the side of the face with a bowl of chocolate pudding. I knew I would either make it or fall on my ass in that split second, so I screwed up my courage and picked up a big plate of spinach and threw it right in Alex Karras' face and we ended up in a free-for-all with food flying through the air and me barricaded under the table. That was my acceptance day. From then on, I was one of the guys."

A few flops followed (does anyone remember *Pieces of Dreams*, *The Gambler* or *Little Fauss and Big Halsey?*) in which Hutton posed prettily. "I didn't understand what I was doing. I hadn't studied. I had this child's fantasy about movies. I thought you came in, the director was the daddy, and he told you what to do and the rest was magic. I thought it would be like going from high school, where everything is lies and junk, to college, where wisdom is dispensed and everything is Oz. I had a rude awakening. I discovered it's so compartmentalized that if you have no credibility they don't want to hear your ideas at all. Most films are like modeling jobs. They hire you and you're supposed to come in a package. That's why most films are bad."

Acting got serious two years ago, when she saw *Nashville* and discovered "something that was different. I sought out Robert Altman, made him an offer he couldn't refuse, and got a job on his crew. I'd been shooting photos on my trips but never showed them to anyone. So I asked him if I could go up to Canada and take still photos on the *Buffalo Bill* location. I got no money, but I learned so much that I got violently excited. It's the first time I ever saw people have fun on a movie set. That's when I got hooked."

In *Gator*, with Burt Reynolds, she played a TV reporter. In *Welcome to L.A.* she played a photographer. In *Viva Knievel* she will play a tough journalist who hopes to get a scoop when Evel kills himself. In Robert Altman's next film, *A Wedding,* she'll be another TV reporter. "I don't know how to play characters yet. All I can do is play little pieces of myself. You have to learn just about everything there is in life to be a good actress. Mostly because of the Revlon image, I get offered rich socialites and glamorous spies. The more living I do, the better I'll be. I'm getting older and smarter."

And she's working on life. In *Viva Knievel* she did her own motorcycle stunts, but the real dangers to that million-dollar face have come from her off-screen adventures. To the horrors of her ulcer-prone bosses at Revlon, she came close to a watery death five months ago while scuba-diving in Australia, forty miles off the Great Barrier Reef. "Second day on the boat the guys strapped on my equipment and I went down eighty feet. The coral was like a wedding cake of pinks, blues, yellows and greens. I got to the bottom and started rolling around in the sand. Suddenly I remembered sick fish do that and make vibrations that attract killer sharks. I looked up and not ten feet away I saw a thirteen-foot whaler shark coming right at me for a direct hit. He had yellow eyes and moved like a locomotive. I didn't even have a penknife and there was no way to run away eighty feet underwater. So I pretended it was a movie, started praying, tried to keep from freaking out or having a coronary, while this monster circled me and made another pass at me with its mouth wide open. Then he went around for the third time and out of the corner of my eye I saw the captain of the boat coming down with his shotgun bomb and we paddled off. Later we got into something really hairy. Shot coral trout and it was trying to get away off the tip of the spear gun when five whaler sharks circled us about six feet away. That was really dangerous, but the only time I was really afraid was when I was alone."

The truth is out. The women buying Ultima II who think they're getting a chunk of Lauren Hutton are buying the wrong image. Glamour is something she leaves to Richard Avedon. The real gal is planning the conclusive, ironic media revenge. "I have this great idea, see, for an underwater commercial with deadly manta rays. It could be for moisturizer. I'd do a water ballet with these creatures and at the end I come up out of the sea and say, 'It's the Ultimate!' Get it? It'd be good for manta rays!"

Critics, beware. She's taking up karate, too.

28

MICHAEL WINNER

HORROR MOVIES, PSYCHOLOGISTS TELL US, ARE JUST ANOTHER visual, vocal and visceral way to tell we're alive. A scream a day keeps the doctor away. The public laps up hair-curling, bone-chilling terror like spaniels devour hamburger. *Rosemary's Baby, The Exorcist, The Omen*—not to mention such low-budget classics as *The Night of the Living Dead* and *The Texas Chainsaw Massacre*—have pumped fresh dividends into Hollywood's empty coffers. Now there's a new horror on the horizon that threatens to break box-office records. It's called *The Sentinel,* and it's hard to believe Michael Winner, the director, is the same man who last year turned out a dumb little dog picture called *Won Ton Ton.*

"It's quite simple, really," he says, sipping Coca-Colas and puffing Cuban cigars in his New York hotel suite while fighting off jet lag from a trans-Atlantic flight. "After *Won Ton Ton,* I certainly wasn't getting any more offers to direct comedies! Besides, I like the idea of frightening people."

Before our meeting, three people had warned me Winner was a feisty egomaniac whose first love was self-promotion. "Ken Russell and I both have that reputation"—he laughs wickedly—"but I think we're both terribly charming! Of course, he raps critics over the head with blunt instruments. I'm too much of a coward. Publicity is good fun. I don't go around knocking on doors to get my name in the paper, but as long as I've got a film I don't mind trying to sell it." The one he's selling now is *The Sentinel.* When he spent Universal's three and a half million dollars quietly last year on location in New York, they didn't say a word. When he showed it to the executives in Hollywood after final editing, they "almost committed suicide by doing a two-foot fall from their padded leather chairs." They asked for a horror film, but they didn't bargain for this.

The Sentinel is about a beautiful model who rents an apartment in a gloomy old building in Brooklyn Heights only to discover it is the gateway to Hell. Corpses come to life, demons ooze and slither through the hallways at midnight, blood splashes across the screen shamelessly, and the audience shrieks its way home to a week of nightmares. Going to bed after seeing *The Sentinel* is like going to bed after a dinner of raw chili peppers and ground glass.

Michael Winner loves the imagery of that. Every scream means dollars in the cash register. "Audiences are fairly unshockable today." He shrugs. "If you're following in the footsteps of *The Exorcist,* where the big scene was a fourteen-year-old girl masturbating with a crucifix, you've got to go some to shock anybody!"

But Winner, who already shocked folks with the realistic rape scene in *Death Wish,* did it again by hiring real freaks from hospitals, freak shows, circuses and asylums to play the devils from Hell. "It took two hours just to make up John Carradine as a blind priest, and he looked like he'd had a rather late night the night before! To do thirty people in makeup with lights melting the wax would've been corny. All it says in the book the movie is based on is 'The armies of Hell rose up.' I didn't want thirty extras with white faces wobbling about. I wanted something spectacularly horrifying! In Marlowe, Dante and the paintings of Hieronymus Bosch, the creatures of Hell were hideously deformed, so I said, 'Let's get the real thing!' Universal knew what I was up to—they got carbons of letters saying, 'Dear Mr. Deformed, please come for an interview at three o'clock'—but they didn't want it publicized."

Freaks have been used before, in Tod Browning's repugnant classic *Freaks*. Brian de Palma used them in *Sisters,* but squeamish execs got cold feet and cut them out of the film. Never has anything like *The Sentinel* been seen by human eyes, however. Some audiences leave the theater raving about the scary makeup, not knowing the truth. Unfortunates with their faces eaten away, goiters, missing eyes and appendages, and worse—they are all here, and one wonders why they did it. "Each one read the script, signed releases and got a promise they could leave if they were offended in any way. There was nothing sensational about it and I have a clear conscience," says Winner. "The remarkable thing is that the creatures we used turned out to be the happiest, most professional group of people I've ever worked with in twenty years of making films. This was their moment in the sun. They photographed each other, got autographs from the stars, they were flown in from everywhere, and it really enriched their lives.

"One man wrote me he had been a recluse who never went out of his home before the film was made because he thought he was the ugliest man in the world. The movie proved to him that there were others worse off than he was. It also had a comic side to it, too. We put them up in hotels during the weekend of the Tall Ships, and the tourists were a bit mortified, I think. Then we gave them chauffeured Cadillacs and the crowds on the set would come around when the cars pulled up, hoping to see Ava Gardner, and out would pop these freaks! They had a sense of humor about it. Nobody had ever asked them to join in life before. Sylvia Miles had to play with them in the nude. Her only complaint was that one of them kept pinching her on the bottom!"

Sylvia Miles also had to munch the brains of a fresh corpse on screen. "It was bread soaked in chemical syrup, and she wasn't really supposed to eat it, but she got carried away and it seemed like such a shame to disturb her. The makeup man whispered to me, 'She's gonna die of food poisoning!' and I said, 'Well, I really don't need her after four o'clock, so it doesn't matter!' She was OK the next day, so she must have a cast-iron stomach!"

Winner has never made a film in a Hollywood studio; everything was an authentic locale. Chris Sarandon's penthouse was really Michael Bennett's apartment on Central Park South. The haunted house was a real building in Brooklyn Heights, inhabited by forty irate tenants who had to be moved into hotels. "One man wanted twenty thousand dollars a day to vacate his room and said if he didn't get it, he'd run an electric saw all day and ruin the sound. We got rid of him by cutting off his electricity in the basement. Another group wanted thirty thousand dollars, which I thought was quite a lot for Brooklyn. So I ignored them. To my horror, I discovered they had a room overlooking the street. When Ava Gardner showed up as the real estate lady to rent the empty house, they hung a sheet in the window. We covered that up with foliage. During the night, they tore down the foliage. This went on for a few weeks, until we invited them to a cast party in the garden—a very boring party, on the cheap, really—but they were so overcome with joy that from then on they were very helpful. We stripped all the furniture, knocked down the walls, and put everything back later. All the tenants did very well in the end. They all got free paint jobs."

If Winner has an ego, it makes good copy. He's not one of those deadly dull directors who go around eating humble pie and boring the press to death because they don't know where their next job is coming from. He's witty, opinionated, quick and, after twenty movies, still full of enthusiasm for the business.

Also, he's candid about the controversial stars he's directed:

☆ Ava Gardner: "I cast her as the realtor in *Sentinel* because every time I rent an apartment in New York I get it from a realtor who looks just like Ava. She keeps saying she's a lousy actress, but she's very good. She's a recluse. She lives near me in an old Victorian house in London and hardly ever goes anywhere or sees anyone. She hardly leads a film-star life, to put it mildly."

☆ Brando, in *The Nightcomers*: "I saw a side of him you don't often see. He was cheerful, dedicated, and worked for no money. That whole film was financed by a rich man for six hundred fifty thousand dollars—a fraction of what Brando usually gets for his salary alone—and he was very loyal to it. He made them delay *Godfather* while he did my picture. He insisted on eating with the crew to prove he wasn't a snob, yet he drove around in limousines with an entourage. Curious contradictions in his character."

☆ Charles Bronson: "We were in Spain, doing *Chato's Land,* and he had to cut the ropes that tied up a naked woman in the desert. He stopped the film and announced, 'I will not appear on the screen with a naked woman!' It was nine P.M. in Almeria, and there was no point arguing. I shot them separately, then edited it together later. Years later, he cornered me and said, 'You still made it look like I was on screen with a naked woman!' Utter nonsense."

☆ Alain Delon, in *Scorpio*: "His English was so poor I asked him to speak slower and he stormed off the set. 'On all my other American pictures, they told me to speak fast so it would look like I understood what I was saying!' he fumed. 'Well,' I said, 'all of your other American pictures were total disasters!' " So was *Scorpio*, which showed, before it was fashionable, the CIA doing naughty things.

A former film critic who came to the fore making dreadful British rock musicals in the early Sixties, Winner has small regard for today's critics. "If a cheap film comes out of Mesopotamia or eastern Bengal showing an Indian peasant climbing two hundred and six steps to get from *A* to *B*, they call the shot one of the greatest camera movements in cinema history, when all it is is five minutes of a man walking upstairs. It's all nonsense and if these films attract an audience of five, it's a big day. Meanwhile, the people in East Bengal don't go to see these bores. They're all going to see American horror movies!"

He says he's unfulfilled because he has yet to make a film that is both artistic and commercial, but he's got this philosophy, and he may be right: "The masses are looking for entertainment, not art. All they want is an hour and a half of light relief in a dark room, and if you don't give it to them you find yourself down the toilet." It's not likely to happen to Michael Winner. As long as audiences demand movies with pow-sock appeal, he's the man who delivers. Critics scoff, but in East Bengal, he's sitting pretty.

29

COMDEN AND GREEN

BETTY COMDEN IS A GENTLE CREATURE WITH REGAL CARRIAGE, terrific cheekbones and a wry smile, who can tilt her head, lower her eyelids and look exactly like Greta Garbo. Adolph Green is a bouncing koala bear with wild white hair like Eskimo fur who gives the impression of being a grinning, enthusiastic Jewish leprechaun. When she is seen about New York in the company of her two children and husband, Steven Kyle, or when he is seen about New York with his two children and wife, Phyllis Newman, they are quite respectable. But when they are together, as they usually are, they are both quite mad.

Luckily for us all, their madness has paid off in the lyrics and books they've written for movies (*Singin' in the Rain, On the Town, Good News, It's Always Fair Weather, The Bandwagon, Auntie Mame, The Berkleys of Broadway*) and Broadway shows (*On the Town, Peter Pan, Two on the Aisle, Wonderful Town, Bells Are*

Ringing, Fade Out–Fade In, Lorelei, Hallelujah, Baby, Subways Are for Sleeping, Do Re Mi, Applause and others too numerous to mention).

Next week, they'll be showing everyone how the stuff they've written is like a party that brightens our lives. They're throwing a party in the shape of a Broadway show in which they'll perform their own songs and satirical sketches. It's called *A Party with Comden and Green* and you don't have to wait for an invitation. Just follow the lines already forming at the Morosco Theatre. For the next few weeks, or at least until their energy gives out, that's where the action will be.

They first performed this party eighteen years ago at a tiny shoe box called the Cherry Lane in Greenwich Village, only a few blocks away from the cellar where they started forty years ago. "We were reluctant," said Adolph the other day in Betty's living room. They always work at Betty's because Phyllis keeps throwing them out when they clutter up the house at Adolph's. "It was going back to where we started and we had worked so long to get uptown above Fourteenth Street. But it was a smash and the Theatre Guild moved us to Broadway. We had to cut short the run because at the time we were in the middle of writing the screenplay for *Bells Are Ringing* with Judy Holliday. We never revived the show after that."

They haven't performed in a show since *On the Town* (1944) but there was always some ham left in them. "Gradually we forgot about performing," says Betty, "and concentrated on making a living."

"The smell of greasepaint does get into your blood," adds Adolph, "but so does the smell of identity." When they went to Hollywood to write *Good News* they used to perform on Saturday nights in Gene Kelly's living room.

One night Leonard Lyons, a visiting New York columnist, came to dinner and Adolph told him not to expect anything special because nothing was happening that night. In walked Humphrey Bogart, Lauren Bacall, Ray Bolger, Ethel Merman, Kay Thompson and Judy Garland. They all performed and sang while Oscar Levant played the piano. Lyons' eyes grew big as obelisks. "Nothin' goin' on, huh?" was his last remark as he staggered into the night.

Their "party" on Broadway will date all the way back to their early revue-sketch days when they were part of an act called The

Revuers. Betty was an NYU student from Brooklyn. Adolph was an "unemployed bum" from the Bronx who once attended City College for one day and later hung around the NYU water fountain, hoping to meet interesting people.

He met Judy Holliday at a summer camp and found her "enchanting, strange and brilliant." While working as a switchboard operator at Orson Welles's Mercury Theatre, Judy got caught in a thunderstorm in Greenwich Village one night and ran for shelter to the doorway of a cellar club called the Village Vanguard, owned by Max Gordon.

"What's a nice kid like you doing in here?" he asked. She said she was looking for work in show business. He asked if she had any talented friends and she told him about Betty and Adolph and they all decided to put on a show. "All of a sudden we got a couple of notices and people started pouring in," laughs Betty. "Lillian Hellman stood in line with Robert Morley. The whole staff of *The New Yorker* came and S. J. Perelman brought Robert Benchley and Ogden Nash. We got five dollars a night and thought we were overpaid."

They call their careers "wildly unplanned." Betty says it all started as a "stopgap" or "something to do while waiting for something big to come along," but it mushroomed. They scribbled ideas on subways, held work meetings to think up new satires on such topics as the *Reader's Digest* and movie ads of the day, and were such an underground sensation that they ended up in the glamorous Rainbow Room, where they bombed.

"Judy and I spent all our time copying the makeup of the Jack Cole dancers who were on the same bill," said Betty. "We were gorgeous but the act was horrible. We ended up back at the Village Vanguard." They also ended up in Hollywood, where The Revuers landed in a Fox musical called *Greenwich Village* with Carmen Miranda. They worked for four months, but when the film was finally released their whole contribution had been reduced to one line, as Betty turned to Don Ameche and said, "Check your hat, sir?" It still haunts her on the late show.

Never fans of Lotus Land, these hard-core New Yorkers look back on their diaper days in the movies with head-shaking humor.

"One day," Betty chuckles, "we all appeared on the set in full makeup and costumes at seven A.M. and the assistant director said,

'OK Revuers, you're through, go home, that's it!' The feeling of being hurled out on the street at dawn with no place to go and the guard at the studio gate no longer smiling—well, that's Hollywood!"

It was the end of the act. Judy Holliday got a movie contract and stayed on. Betty went home to see her future husband, Steve, who was being shipped overseas by the Army. Adolph followed soon after. She met him at Grand Central with a sign reading "ADOLPH GREEN FAN CLUB" (a scene movie buffs will recognize, since they later used it in *The Bandwagon*) and soon after that, Adolph's old roommate Leonard Bernstein came up with the idea of turning his ballet *Fancy Free* into a Broadway musical. They called it *On the Town* and you know the rest.

They've been writing shows ever since. Most were hits, but they've had their Gethsemanes, too. One was called *Bonanza Bound*. "It was about the Alaskan gold rush," says Adolph. "That was our first mistake. You cannot do a musical about the Alaskan gold rush unless it stars Groucho Marx. Ours starred George Coulouris, which was our second mistake. The only good thing that came out of that was a chorus girl named Gwen Verdon."

But now they've just completed a new musical, starring Madeleine Kahn, with music by Cy Coleman, based on the movie classic *Twentieth Century*, which will hit Broadway next season. They meet every day and toss new ideas around.

"We have enormous frustrations because neither of us can write music, and we're full of musical ideas. Working so often with Jule Styne and Leonard Bernstein, who are great friends as well as geniuses, we've developed a kind of musical shorthand. We barely knew Cy Coleman, but the first time we sat down to write something with him things began to happen. He had imagination, individuality and a head full of exciting musical ideas. He's fast and prolific, and the new score is just glorious. It's given us a new enthusiasm for working in the musical theater again. All of our ideas bled off into each other, and that's what a good collaboration is."

They get hung up on words when they describe their working process. Sometimes the music comes first, sometimes a completed lyric comes first and music is composed to fit it later. Adolph calls the mysterious work process "an unconscious give-and-take." Betty calls it "mental radar." Sometimes they come up with a title or a melody in the show to fit it.

"Betty can work at seven A.M. but I can't. I'm a night person," says Adolph, who isn't himself till noon.

"So we've learned to give, and adjust to each other's patterns," adds Betty sweetly, "—which means we work late."

Sometimes they get "eureka moments" when songs burst forth, just like Mickey Rooney and Tom Drake in the movies. At other times, they get so depressed they wonder if Stephen Sondheim would write it better.

They've written for stars like Frank Sinatra, Gene Kelly, Mary Martin, Phil Silvers, Nancy Walker, June Allyson, Carol Burnett and Bert Lahr. Rosalind Russell was the hardest, because she told them, going into *Wonderful Town,* that she couldn't dance and had a range of four notes. "We found a way to get around that by structuring everything to her own talents. Instead of teaching her how to dance a whole production number, Jerome Robbins said 'Roz, just improvise something and I'll teach the rest of the company to follow.' She was a great clown and she did some awkward kicks and the whole chorus imitated her and the result was a song called the 'Wrong Note Rag' which stopped the show. There's a way around everything when you have a great star like that."

They've been lucky. Movies have changed. There will probably never be any more great Comden and Green musicals for MGM. Trying to make *Singin' in the Rain* today would cost $30 million just to talk about it. Also, they aren't training any new musical stars to take the place of yesterday's giants like Judy Holliday, Judy Garland, Bert Lahr, Fred Astaire or Gene Kelly.

Even the future of Broadway musicals is in serious jeopardy. But Comden and Green are like those tireless, enthusiastic, stagestruck kids in old Mickey Rooney movies.

Got a barn going to waste? They'll write a show for it. And the great thing is, they have the last word. If nobody else sings the songs they write, they can always sing them themselves. They throw the best *Party* in town.

Susan Sarandon PARAMOUNT PICTURES CORP.

Geraldine Page

John Schlesinger

Michael Winner

**Betty Comden and
Adolph Green**

Chita Rivera (with dancers Frank Mastrocola and Michael Serrecchia)

BILL ANDERSON

Susan Clark PHOTO © MICHAEL CHILDERS/SYGMA

Jon Voight

ROGER VARGO

Diane Keaton PARAMOUNT PICTURES CORP.

30

CHITA RIVERA

SHE LEAPS. SHE JUMPS. SHE SLICES BREAKFAST MELON, KNOCKING over a personally engraved cigarette lighter from Neil Diamond with his autograph in gold. She pours coffee and dances at the same time. Chita Rivera's movements, even at a ridiculously early morning hour, are big and sassy. I don't know how old she is, but as she prepares for her big nightclub solo at the chic Waldorf's Empire Room, it is obvious that she has swallowed the Fountain of Youth.

On Broadway, she's pow-socko-boom! Now she's spreading out, reaching new audiences, raising her name to its proper place in lights. Theatergoers have applauded Chita Rivera for years in shows like *West Side Story, Sweet Charity, Bye Bye, Birdie* and *Chicago.* Now the rest of the world is getting a look, and the view is sublime.

She just returned from Las Vegas, where she was an opening act for Engelbert Humperdinck (the sophisticated Sardi's set is still holding its nose over that one!) and now she's headlining the bill on a cross-country tour that will keep her in Capezios for the next year. "Listen," she says, directing part of her fabulous Bob Mackie wardrobe toward the ironing board between ringing phones and noisy doorbells that announce more congratulatory telegrams from the legends of show business, "this club act all started when rehearsals for *Chicago* were halted because of Bob Fosse's heart attack. We were out of work, so I gathered some of the kids together and started working on an act to keep busy. Now it's changed the entire course of my life.

"We got rave reviews in New York, then took the show to Los Angeles and they came out of the woodwork! One night I had Lina Wertmuller, Giancarlo Giannini, Lana Turner and Paul Lynde all in the same room! The act is bringing me new audiences.

"If you're a hard-core theater person from Broadway musicals, there's a large area of the country that never knows who you are unless you're on TV. Those pregnant ladies who stuff nickels in slot machines never get to Broadway. I don't want to just dance for my best friends. I've got enough best friends already."

She didn't even mind opening the show for a mediocrity like Humperdinck. "The screaming fans who came to watch his pants rip didn't know what a Chita Rivera was, honey. But they found out. It was a great chance. He was a doll and a gentleman, but his pants were so tight he couldn't move.

"I used to tease him by saying, 'You know, your buns are supposed to move separately!' But it's all show business. I got standing ovations from people from Kansas and Oklahoma who never heard of me in their lives. I was scared to death, too. It's a crazy town. Las Vegas still sounds funny to me. After three weeks there, we were putting our faces in chocolate cake. You get desert fever. You get crazy because there's nothing to do, no streets to walk on.

"I got back to New York, and even the doggie-doo smelled good. I did feel like an elephant act, but somebody said to me, 'You're gonna be back in Vegas, honey, and you'll be rolling in money!' I think it was Raquel Welch. That girl is so gorgeous you could crack her face!"

With everything she does, there's the humor that shines through like new sunshine on a foggy moor. She's had to summon it on occasion just to survive the narrow-mindedness of typecasting. For years, everyone called her a taco or a tamale. Every role for a spitfire or a peasant girl dancing around a campfire would go to the girl with the Latin name.

"After a while you get used to being called a bombshell. Hello. That's not bad. Words like fireworks and explosive aren't bad. That's better than having the critics say, 'Here comes Miss Vanilla Pudding again.' I just always figured it was better to keep working. As a creative person, I've got to be creative, or I rot. Even between shows, when I wasn't working, I'd go back to ballet class or teach dancing in high schools. I can't be idle. I have too much energy. Even if I choose the wrong thing to do, I've gotta do it."

And she's chosen some clinkers. Does anybody remember *Zenda* with Alfred Drake? "That one," she roars, "was better than a show called *1491.* John Cullum was Christopher Columbus, and at the end of the show he discovered America with something that looked like the steering wheel from a toy scooter. It had costumes for days, we opened in Pasadena and I played a Spanish Jewess—naturally—a barefoot wench who came in the back door and hissed at the queen. My friends said, 'Oh, Chita, we don't know how to tell you this,' and I said, 'You already have.' It was so terrible I have to laugh when I think of it. It was just one of many Latin hussies I've played."

Half the world thinks she's Cuban; the other half thinks she's from Tijuana. To clear up the mystery, she's a mixture of Puerto Rican and Scottish from Washington, D.C. Her father was a saxophone player in the Harry James Orchestra, and her real name is Dolores Concita Figueroa del Rivero. "With a name like that on the marquee, you'd have to wear a mantilla and carry a rose in your teeth.

"Ben Bagley made me change my name when I was in the *Shoestring Revue.* I was mad about Maureen O'Hara, so for three weeks I was Chita O'Hara. Friends would call up, say 'Chita W-h-a-t?' and hang up. It found its way to Chita Rivera. Now I have absolutely no feeling about seeing my name up in lights. It scares the hell outta me."

She lets out a banshee hoot when anyone calls her a star. The word does not exist in her vocabulary. "Mickey Mouse and Donald Duck are stars. They cannot be replaced. I don't even know what a live human star is. I've always been a gypsy, one of the kids in the chorus. That's the difference between the Broadway mentality of people like Gwen Verdon and me—dedication, hard work and the development of a craft—and the Hollywood mentality, which is really a job and out of it sometimes comes fame. I couldn't care less about being a movie star.

"I learned not to be too disappointed or count on Hollywood when I watched my role in *Bye Bye, Birdie* go to Janet Leigh, my role in *West Side Story* go to Rita Moreno. I did finally make a picture when Bob Fosse used me in *Sweet Charity,* and I had enough of picture-making. There is nothing in the world to replace the live stage.

"I never thought much about my career. It just sort of happened. I didn't have time to plan it because I was always too busy working. All I ever wanted to do was dance. I was trained from the age of eleven to be a ballet dancer, and one day I went to an audition with a friend and ended up in *Call Me Madam* and Jerome Robbins was the choreographer. That led to other shows, and all the kids cutting their teeth at the same time were people like Sheldon Harnick, Shirley MacLaine, Carolyn Leigh, Dody Goodman, Jerry Herman, Bea Arthur, Arte Johnson, Carol Burnett. I feel so sorry for kids today. They can't possibly have that kind of training. There's no place for dancers to work."

Chita's own daughter, Lisa Mordente, is now a budding musical star herself. Chita and child recently did a flaming version of "America" on "The Merv Griffin Show" together, and Chita was so excited she could hardly remember her own dance steps. "It all flashed back. I was doing the same number for *West Side Story* for five months while I was carrying Lisa in my stomach, and here I was doing the same number with her as a grown-up woman while her daddy, Tony Mordente, was directing her. It was unbelievable. She and Liza Minnelli are best friends, and they sound exactly alike. I feel like I'm reliving the past through them."

There's not much show-biz talk at Chita's house. She won't let Lisa play her records. She likes to do it, not talk about it. She does needlepoint, she makes a terrific lasagna, and she eats no meat. "I also stay away from lettuce because it retains water, eat bran every morning and take ten thousand units of Vitamin C, E and B daily. Sometimes I fall off the wagon and have three banana splits in a row."

She has been remarkably lucky as a dancer, with relatively few injuries, although she did throw her calf out of joint in *Can-Can* and fell on her knee in *Sweet Charity* and still suffers pain from those old injuries.

"Age is the enemy of all dancers. They don't talk about it, but it's there. You cannot dance forever. There comes a time beyond which the muscles don't work. My knee injury sometimes swells up like a lump, and it could turn into arthritis, who knows? I can't do thirty-two fouettés or four pirouettes in a row like I used to. My technique is slipping. But I'm strong and I love what I'm doing. That keeps my muscles in better shape than most people. But I know I can't dance forever, so I'm gradually moving into other areas of acting.

"That old saw about how you don't sing, you dance—or you don't say lines, you dance—well, that's changing. Now you have to be able to do everything. It's sad that when Gwen and I go, there's nobody to take over.

"But I keep my mind clear, young and progressive. That, combined with the right exercise, makes my body move easier. And"—she winks, and you know the "and" is a big one—"if age does catch up with me, you find me planting zinnias. I'm going to be one Latin bombshell who's gonna be a swinging old lady!"

31

SUSAN CLARK

EVERYONE KNOWS SUSAN CLARK AS BABE DIDRIKSON ZAHARIAS, Amelia Earhart, Hedda Gabler, Lady Macbeth and Colette. But nobody knows Susan Clark. Good reason. For ten years, she's been buried under one of those "We'll make you a star" contracts at Universal. It took her a minute to say yes. It took her a decade to claw her way out. Now she's free. "School's out," she says softly. "Now I can do anything I want, or nothing at all." What she's got is what she'd get at the end of ten years in analysis—herself. But who is she?

The elegant blonde is a horse in midstream, and she's got the shapely legs to carry her anywhere she chooses to go. They seem to start at her navel. It is no wonder that her professional debut was in *Silk Stockings*. But that's getting ahead of the story. She comes from Toronto. Her father was a football player. At the age of nine, she was taking acting lessons. By the age of twelve, she was a full-fledged member of the Toronto Children's Theatre, where she was guided by Raymond Massey's sister, Dorothy Goulding. At fifteen, she was apprenticing in summer stock. With money saved, she fled to England at seventeen, enrolled at the Royal Academy of Dramatic Art, lost her North American accent, and debuted on the London stage with

Donald Pleasance in *Poor Bitos.* When her father died of cancer in 1965, Susan returned to Canada, starred in an award-winning production of "Heloise and Abelard" on TV, which led to a meeting with talent scouts Eleanor Kilgallen and Monique James, who ran Universal Studios' "talent development" program. Susan headed for Hollywood to become a star. She was twenty-three years old.

Universal has always had a bunch of girls wasting away under seven-year contracts. They usually wait at the fort in gingham skirts while the male stars fight the Apaches. Susan turned in consistently strong performances in junky movies where her co-stars got the close-ups. Some of her leading men were Richard Widmark, Clint Eastwood, Burt Lancaster, Burt Reynolds, Rock Hudson, Gene Hackman and Robert Redford. Except for *Tell Them Willie Boy Is Here,* they were all forgettable. When Susan crosses those Cyd Charisse legs and ponders the wasteful ten years she's just been through, it sounds like a case of too much talent in the wrong sausage factory.

"I was in a stable," she says. "Tall, skinny, with cheekbones, and scared to death. For the first five years, I didn't know what I was doing there. I kept notebooks on the characters I played, did homework on character analysis, asked a million questions. I was saying, 'Hey, can I come on your trip, because I'm a little nervous on mine.' I wanted to contribute and share. The directors patted me on the head and said, 'That's nice,' and none of it ever came off on the screen. Nobody ever said, 'Schmuck, what are you wasting your time for?' An identity crisis developed, I ended up on an analyst's couch."

She was too well-trained and overqualified for the shock-shlock Universal wanted to use her for. Her credentials were too good. In 1970, she went on a long suspension for refusing to do any more tacky work. "I became a recluse. I lost my perspective and my sense of humor. I was so-o-o-o naïve. I had been a tunnel-vision person. I'd been superbly trained at seventeen at the Royal Academy. I'd done fifty plays on the stage before I was twenty-one. It didn't mean shit in California. In fact, I pretended it didn't happen. I tried to hide my own talent and my own intelligence. I thought it would be too embarrassing to let anyone know I had played *Taming of the Shrew* and *Mary of Scotland* on the Universal back lot. In all those years, they never found a way to market me. If they could do it with a can of soup, why couldn't they do it with an attractive, eager young actress?"

She hid out, married and divorced a writer named Robert Joseph, and the next shot out of the bag was a part in *The Skin Game* playing a "nice hooker-pickpocket named Ginger. The Universal executives said, 'Jeez, we didn't know you could be sexy and funny, too.' Then nothing happened." Next came a western called *Showdown* with Rock Hudson and Dean Martin. "I didn't carry any bandages for the wounded gunfighters in that one, but I fed the chickens back at the ranch while they fought each other." Defeated and depressed, she went off and became the youngest woman ever to play Lady Macbeth in a triumphant production at the Seattle Repertory Company.

Impressed, Universal renegotiated her contract for more money, promising bigger parts. "Every one came out like another very good cake mix. This one's chocolate, that one's lemon. I finally freaked out, stopped fighting the system and said, 'Please let me out of here!' Find someone else who can turn out cake mixes graciously and with excitement! I could not and would not be a television star!" Then she contradicted herself, because the first thing she did after refusing to appear in a TV series was the TV special "Babe," for which she won a treasured Emmy award. "But that was easy. For the first time, I felt nurtured, protected. All of my opinions, contributions, foibles, eccentricities—everything was used! They said 'Terrific, give us more!' Five hours a day running my ass off at the UCLA track and three hours a day playing golf was easy because my energy finally had a focus. What was difficult for me at Universal was the lack of focus and the feeling of always walking on quicksand."

She won another Emmy nomination for "Amelia Earhart," in which her performance as the lost-aviatrix heroine was so impressive it cost Shirley MacLaine and Pete Hamill a whole movie they were preparing on the same subject. Susan Clark was finally getting the applause she had worked for so arduously at Universal.

She obtained her freedom in September. Since then, she has completed a TV production of "Hedda Gabler" and signed for another TV special based on the life of legendary French writer Colette, to be directed by Frank Perry, a man who will know exactly what to do with the talent others have overlooked. She has a new movie for Walt Disney called *The North Avenue Irregulars*, in which she plays a law-abiding church lady who forms a league of women crime fighters to confront the Mafia in their New York suburb. Next, she goes into *The Diviners*, playing the daughter of a Canadian garbage collector in the Manitoba wilderness who has a child by an Indian savage. Next summer, she plans to tour with her "Babe" co-star Alex Karras in a stage production of *Born Yesterday*, revealing yet another comic side of her untapped resources. Karras, the former Detroit Lion tackle they nicknamed "Mr. Mean," is also the man in her life. Her father was a football player. Now she's in love with another one. She's come full circle.

"I think I really fell in love with him because he never tested me," she says. "I was raised to believe a real woman should have a mink coat, two kids and a station wagon by the age of thirty. I didn't have any of those things when I met Alex. I never heard of him before we met on the 'Babe' set. I had undergone a lot of emotional pain to get free from Universal in order to do that show and I was going into his world—a non-sports person in a movie about sports people. I still have muscles from throwing the javelin. It could have been an impossible situation, but Alex was instantly supportive and sympathetic and wonderful. He didn't make me feel insecure because I was intelligent. It's a disadvantage to be intelligent in Hollywood. It's even worse to show it. I never could understand why being attractive and bright was a threat. Men were always saying, 'You're too smart!' and I kept thinking, Does that mean we can't be friends? When you're younger, it's necessary to prove you can act, to prove you're a real woman, to prove, prove, prove. Now I don't have to prove anything, I just have to do it."

Now that she's an independent success whose talent is being justifiably applauded, Susan says she can't remember what she did with her time all those years. "I've got to find out if, after all those movies and TV shows, I still want to act. I don't care about pleasing anybody but myself. I feel strung out. I've been through the machine, I've come out with all the limbs intact, and I can't honestly say there were any villains. They pacified me. They treated me like a talented, difficult child. And I learned a lot. I snooped around in the Universal files, read books they owned, found ideas for parts I wanted to play, screened their old movies. I think I could be a pretty good producer on my own. They even sent me to Washington as a token woman to speak to the FCC on behalf of family-choice cable TV. They once let me spend six months developing a script on the life of Victoria Woodhull, which they never made. I've been wounded by the chaos in my career, but it's all over now. I don't have to worry about images or the way I look. I've learned to trust. Falling in love with Alex

Karras coincided with my release from Universal, so I'm not starting all over on my own. I've got a great guy to share my freedom with. Just call me a knowledgeable beginner."

Or late-blooming survivor. Whatever the role, Susan Clark can play it. She learned the hard way, and nothing can stop her now.

32

JOHN SCHLESINGER

JOHN SCHLESINGER BEAMS LIKE A DISNEY COW. THE NOTICES ARE in on *Marathon Man,* the season's big movie blockbuster, and it's going to make him rich. Last year, he directed *The Day of the Locust*, and it rained on his parade. How can you win? He made a great film, and some critics said he should have stayed in bed. Now he makes a totally commercial escapist thriller, and some critics are saying it's beneath his dignity.

How does a John Schlesinger keep from going crazy? "Well," he says, rubbing circles on his bald head, "you just laugh. I'm happy *Marathon Man* is a hit, but that doesn't make me any less proud of *Locust*. You just have to do what interests you in life and plunge ahead. I went through similar frustrations after *Far from the Madding Crowd*. It was a disaster. I followed it with *Midnight Cowboy*, and everyone said, 'Why do you want to do such a depressing film that nobody will ever go and see?' Then that one was an enormous success, and that was the moment I was offered a lot of very big pictures to direct. Instead, I did *Sunday Bloody Sunday* because it seemed like the right movie to make.

"The answer is that since every director's career is going to be a checkered one, and we can't all have hits all the time, we have to take chances. We no longer live in a golden era in which directors went under contract to a studio that guaranteed a certain amount of work each year. In the Forties, a director never had to worry about where the next film was coming from. You just made films, one after the other, some good, some bad. That's how all the great reputations were made. Now it's a big gamble, and every time you make a film, your whole future is at stake. That's why I'm always anxious to get the next one prepared while the old one is being released."

He pours tea in a most civilized British manner while the phone rings angrily. The newspaper ads are spread on the sofa, pronouncing *Marathon Man* the greatest thing since peanut butter. Studio executives are trying to break through with offers that go ignored. Schlesinger is king of the mountain. There's nothing like lines around the block under the marquee to ensure self-confidence. Yet he seems nervous.

"I shall never stop being anxious." He sighs. "I'm always on the edge of a precipice, ready for the deep end. I'm a nervous wreck. I'm always scared because one's success and failure these days is so rapidly judged on what the film will gross. There were people going around after *Day of the Locust* saying, 'He must never be allowed near a camera again.' There's nothing you can do except shrug and carry on. The main thing is to cash in at the moment you have a commercial success and use that power to do a film that would not have a chance otherwise.

"*Sunday Bloody Sunday* will never show a profit, although it had huge critical acclaim. You can't make movies for critics, or you will destroy yourself. On the other hand, that film would never have been made if it had not been for the commercial success of *Midnight Cowboy*. Francis Coppola did the same thing. After *The Godfather* he used his muscle to make *The Conversation*, which was not a commercial success, but the right move to make. In this business, one must take risks to remain a creative artist.

"Now with the success of *Marathon Man*, I am taking advantage of my sudden popularity to make a film in England called *Yanks!*, a love story about an American G.I. and an English girl just before

D-Day. It's a kind of funny, touching, raunchy script by a young writer from the North Country of England, and we're currently going around New York meeting men who were in England during the war. I'm not making any more adventure thrillers or heist movies. I'm going back to my roots."

"Coming from England, where the economy is so unstable that it is impossible to get any kind of movie produced, do you think American actors who get a million dollars per film are overpaid?" I asked.

"Dustin Hoffman certainly got it for *Marathon Man* and the studio thought he was worth it, but I look at it all with a jaundiced eye. I certainly did not come to America to make a profit. I like America, and I've been coming here since I was a student. I'm hooked on the place. But I came to make *Midnight Cowboy*. Then I went back home to make *Sunday* and came back to make *Locust*. It took me years to get that one off the ground, and I had to work on it in Hollywood, so I bought a house there, and now my tax situation is absolutely chaotic.

"But I've also had projects that never got off the ground at all. I developed Evelyn Waugh's *Handful of Dust* with my own money, and nobody wanted to make it. Then I was planning to make *Alive!* but the Stigwood people came out with a total rip-off in that dubbed Mexican atrocity called *Survive!* which is truly a piece of crap. But it ruined my film because the story has now been told. Now *Marathon Man* is a great smash and that pleases me, but I wouldn't call it my favorite film."

It was certainly different. He had no experience with the enormity of that kind of film, but he tackled it anyway by "depending a lot on the technical experts around me—the designers, stunt coordinators, special unit director, cameraman, special-effects men, everybody. They all played a great part in it. For me, a film is always a collaboration. I can't take credit for all of it. In the middle of all the car crashes and explosions, I did have to find a way to establish an individual touch of my own. That was the hard part.

"I remember walking around New York with Bill Goldman, the writer, and it was Yom Kippur. I suddenly got an idea. Since the first car crash involved an old Jew and an old Nazi, why not set it on Yom Kippur? That was the first bit of texture that occurred to me. Then in Paris when we were scouting locations, we were having a script conference in a hotel room at the Plaza-Athénée. Suddenly there was a noise outside, and it was a political rally. People came out on their balconies to watch. Another idea was born. What would happen if we had Roy Scheider attacked by the murderous villain while he's watching a street demonstration from his hotel window? It's little things like that that make films different.

"The biggest problem with *Marathon Man* was how to blend the elements of melodrama—Nazi torturers, villains, explosions, chases—and keep the film on a realistic level. In most thrillers, whole masses of people go in a matter of seconds to all sorts of comic deaths, and nobody takes it seriously because nobody feels anything. *Marathon Man* is different because it happens to an innocent person, and the audience is identifying like mad.

"I don't know if I want to do another film like this. Up to now, all of my films have been about small people and real relationships, but I wanted a change. I believe in change. I admire Hitchcock, but I don't know how he's been able to make the same movie over and over again without feeling the need for change. This was my first thriller, Dustin Hoffman's first thriller, Bill Goldman's first thriller, and for two weeks of rehearsal we were always asking logical questions about the plot. Finally, Goldman just said, 'It's a thriller, for God's sake! You just have to believe it!' And that's when I decided it would only work if we treated it just as seriously as Chekhov."

Rumors persisted during filming that there were problems with Dustin Hoffman. True or false? "Well, there were differences, but they don't show on the screen. Dustin is one of those actors who asks a million questions, and then wants take after take after take, and you just have to say no very firmly and call a halt. Laurence Olivier, on the other hand, is very precise, doesn't like to improvise, and just wants to get on with it. His patience was severely tried, but luckily he liked Dustin and they got along. Olivier can't remember his lines the way he used to because of his recent illness, but Dustin required just as many retakes. It all evened out."

And what about line producer Robert Evans, who has taken his share of credit for the film's success? "Bob found the book, came to me and helped every inch of the way. I didn't want Dustin. I thought he was too old. I wanted an unknown. Evans begged me to reconsider. So we made a pact that we'd never mention his age in the film. Evans came up with the idea of Olivier. I thought he was too ill to work. Evans pressured me into using big-star names. Then when we started shooting, we had some differences. The film was not well organized, Bob couldn't understand why I wanted a lot of garbage littering the streets of Paris—little things. But all good producers—and there aren't many—have as their first concern the film itself.

"Not until we were in the cutting room did I realize what a remarkable, tasteful man Robert Evans is. I was deceived by the eye-catching, glamorous lifestyle he likes to advertise. When he was head of the studio, he hated *Day of the Locust*. He opposed it every step of the way, and there was a lot of animosity between us. But when he saw it, he said he didn't like it and it wouldn't make a dime, but felt it was very well directed. Then he asked if there was anything I had cut out that I would like to put back. That surprised me. That was the first time I knew how much he respected directors. The second time was when I went to talk to him about *Marathon Man*, and he was on the phone fighting with the labs over the color processing on *Chinatown*. Then I knew he was much more than just a playboy.

"We developed an extremely close relationship. I know people regard him as a figure of fun, but he's amazingly acute. He really made hundreds of valuable contributions. He was an objective eye and ear, and I trusted his advice completely."

A chauffeur arrives to glide him to his next appointment. He pauses. "However . . ." The word has an ominous ring. "I don't think Bob Evans is prepared to take the same kind of risk I am with material. He would never have made *Sunday Bloody Sunday*. He only wants to make films that are big commercial blockbusters. I am glad we have a commercial blockbuster with *Marathon Man*. But in the final analysis"—he crooks his head, half-Cheshire cat, half-homeless waif, like a man who has his cake but doesn't feel sustained because it isn't pie—"I don't think that's the way to make pictures."

33

JON VOIGHT

SEEKING PERFECTION IN THE MOVIES IS LIKE HAVING A TASTE FOR caviar in the tuna-fish industry, but Jon Voight is a determined cuss. He's a friendly, modest man with integrity and intelligence, but you sense his will is as strong as his jawline. He will be forty next year but appears younger in *Coming Home*, the new film for which he's getting the kind of attention he got ten years earlier, when he burst upon the screen in *Midnight Cowboy*. In both, he shattered his boy-next-door image by playing against type, with a rigid determination to be different. "In all of my work there's been a loneliness, but audiences seem to respond to me best when I play one man against the world with his sensuality untapped."

Rubbing the sleep from his eyes while wolfing down scrambled eggs on an early Saturday morning, Voight *is* in person what he tries to be on the screen—a master at character disguise. Long hair demolishes the image of the captain of the basketball team, and a scraggly beard hides the smooth contours of his well-bred face. Only the blue eyes, always direct, are a dead giveaway. They shine brightly, as out of place in the funky frame of his rumpled face as store-bought marbles on a Harlem sidewalk.

"My looks have always limited me," he says ruefully. "I came along at a time when blond, American WASPs were on their way out and ethnic punks were on their way in. The new guys are from the Bogart-Garfield-Cagney school. I'm more related to Gary Cooper and Randolph Scott, but those roles aren't around to play. When I came on the scene the kind of compassion and open-faced honesty I have were no longer in vogue. We were going through a critical period politically and socially so people were suspicious of people who looked like me. The anti-hero was born and I didn't look like an anti-hero.

"Now I get a lot of Clint Eastwood scripts. I don't understand that kind of character and I don't agree with those movies. I've always thought of myself as a romantic, lyric type. That's why I got the role in *Coming Home*. That character wouldn't work if he wasn't a man who needed love. For the past fifteen years leading men have been tough, cool, neurotic, dangerous. Then Vietnam taught us men could cry, men could be vulnerable. Now a new man is emerging. Stallone in *Rocky* was a sweetheart. Bill Holden in *Network* kept the picture together. Maybe my time is coming. I just can't play invulnerable men with any finesse."

In *Coming Home*, he plays a paraplegic who learns to live again through the tenderness and affection of a lonely war bride, played by Jane Fonda. For nine weeks, he lived among the paraplegics in the Rancho Los Amigos Hospital in Los Angeles.

"I was originally offered the Bruce Dern part of the brain-damaged husband who comes back emotionally scarred but with his body intact. I wanted to play the guy in the wheelchair. It's impossible for me to accept any role without enthusiasm. There's an awful lot of silly stuff around and I knew I could make this character live. All of us had different viewpoints on what kind of a movie we wanted to make. Sometimes Jane won and sometimes I won. But we all wanted to tell the truth about Vietnam and still have a movie about people, not politics. It was the veterans in the hospital who provided the real truth for me. They fed me all of the information I needed. I ate with them, lived with them, remained in my wheelchair the whole time. If I walked, I did it late at night when nobody was around.

"Their first reaction to the film was that they wanted something said, but didn't trust anyone to say it in a movie. I had to earn their trust. They were tough, but they learned to accept me as one of them. I am one of them! They're like my brothers.

"Their reaction to Jane was different. The hawks respected her for her political opinions but didn't think she knew what she was talking about. Then when she came to the set, they all forgot about her political history and concentrated on her sex appeal. At the end of the film, they all liked her. We had a big wrap party and Jane made a touching speech. One of the editors cut together thirty minutes of the footage the paraplegics were in and they went crazy. It was their film. Jane and I were just extras walking through the background. Two best buddies got drunk and broke each other's noses in a fist fight in wheelchairs and the whole thing was wild."

Coming Home takes place in 1968, the year of the Tet Offensive, the assassinations of Bobby Kennedy and Martin Luther King, the Democratic convention. It was the year Voight was busy making *Midnight Cowboy*, the film that rocketed him to stardom. "In the States, the war was in the streets. We were being polarized as Americans, and I wanted to do something. So I went to the Chicago Seven trials and met Tom Hayden and got shocked into an awareness of what was going on. Here was a group of young people who were saying, 'We won't let you commit atrocities in our names!' and the older Establishment, which was saying, 'We'll destroy you if you try to be different!' and both sides were very close to violence.

"From my own limited knowledge of the war, I went to Washington with Candy Bergen and Joe Papp and we staged a sit-down protest on the floor of the Senate and got jailed. Then Jane Fonda came back from Vietnam and showed me some films and I was just horrified. So I staged lectures anywhere people would give us a building, and we had slide shows to try to educate people to what was going on, and tried to get the people in the film industry involved. People were frightened of losing their jobs. It was slow going, but I felt more like a citizen than I've ever felt in my life. There were FBI agents following us and taking notes on us. Then I enlisted in the McGovern campaign and made speeches on campuses. I tried to do what I could.

"I wasn't as good at it as Jane. I'm always seeking more information. Jane just plows right in. She has a tremendous ability to commit herself totally to the moment and not think about the past or any ramifications in the future. On *Coming Home* she came to the set totally prepared, dropped the mother role she played that morning getting her kids to school, worked as a professional actress, then during the lunch break she would make all of her phone calls to set up her projects for solar energy or whatever else she was into. Then, when she left the set, she would go on to the next person she is. She has total energy. I've never been able to do that. I go from job to job, pulling all of these loads behind me, trying to figure out who I am."

The search led him to a dead standstill four years ago, when he dropped out of films after a debacle called *The End of the Game*, directed by Maximilian Schell and co-starring Jacqueline Bisset. "I did it because Max Schell and Jackie were godparents to one of my kids. I tend to make families out of actors very quickly and sometimes I lend my contributions to their projects without making personal demands. My reticence to protect my work in the stuff I've chosen to do is one of my flaws. I haven't gotten angry enough. I had just done another clinker, *The Odessa File*, and it was a bad time for me psychologically. I just wasn't able to see what was going on objectively. By the time I realized my career was falling apart, it was almost too late. People kept saying, 'You can't go through life looking for another *Midnight Cowboy*,' so I started giving in to commercial pressures and I was not doing my best work."

At the same time, his father died, his wife's mother died, his marriage was rocky and he had a lot of things on his mind. "I just had to get out of the movie business for a while and re-think. Luckily I had some money from *Deliverance* that held me together. So I made a decision to be a better actor instead of a rich actor." He turned down shlock movies, did *Hamlet* at Rutgers University to less than ecstatic reviews, tackled Stanley Kowalski in a Los Angeles production of *A Streetcar Named Desire* with Faye Dunaway, a role for which he was neither physically nor emotionally suited. It was a courageous failure, but he was "learning all the time." He went back to acting class, worked on problems and hangups, became his toughest critic.

His own ambitions now? "The money's run out; I'm real low on funds, I've got to make another film to support my family. As this time in my children's lives, I don't want to go away to Pago Pago for a year. The public seems to respond to me in sensitive leading roles, but I still don't want to be type-cast."

He's written a script based on an idea he got from his brother, who is a handicapper at Aqueduct, about a wacky gambler, which he describes as "a combination of *Midnight Cowboy*, Laurel and Hardy, and Fellini." But his real dream is to play a vampire and he's got a secret project in mind that is "the *Gone With the Wind* of monster pictures."

Meanwhile, there's the success of *Coming Home* to bask in. "When I look at it, I have to say we achieved something that is quite splendid. The energy is positive, and I can see my contribution on the screen. I was working with people who cared, who were hungry to put their stamp on something meaningful. I did not cheat. For me, it examines that period of the Vietnam war in terms of feelings we didn't know we had. We were being separated from each other, that was the American tragedy. This film gives us back a belief in ourselves, restores our self-respect. If we can be clear and critical and accept what we did in Vietnam—which we must—we can somehow gain strength from it."

A smile cracks through the beard like new sun. Maybe a vampire could look like the captain of an Ivy League basketball team.

34

DIANE KEATON

WHO IS THIS CHAPLINESQUE CREATURE SHLEPPING DOWN FIRST Avenue in the rain? Baggy pants, well-cut hacking jacket, and bowler hat. Coming through the door. It's Keaton! No, not Buster, dummy. Diane! A movie star. See, she looks just as she does in Woody Allen's colossal blockbuster *Annie Hall*. She's wearing the same sunglasses even though it's pouring rain. If the street-smart waitress in Diane's neighborhood greasy-spoon coffee shop thought I was meeting a movie star, she never blinked. Glazed, she plunked down the ubiquitous plastic glass of New York ice water and stared at Keaton as if she were a teen-age runaway.

In days before movies, the warmly shy and gently reticent actress might've been a beloved, reclusive poetess like Emily Dickinson, or a repressed but daring novelist like Katherine Mansfield, whose artistic talent might have led more to the shallows of obscure eccentricity than the peaks of fame and fortune. Today, however, there's no doubt that Miss Keaton is standing in the shadow of stardom as surely as *Annie Hall* is cleaning up at the box office. Word is already out that she is merely magnificent in Richard Brooks's screen version of the best-selling shocker *Looking for Mr. Goodbar*.

Safely tucked on the edge of a leather booth, Diane observes the world through her rose-colored glasses and removes her cowboy hat, releasing a fall of fine, shiny ginger-colored hair instantly tamed by being tucked into her jacket collar. Black coffee is all she wants. Amid the clatter of chipped cups and saucers, her laughter is quiet but infectious. "I don't understand stardom very much, you know. One should have the responsibility to do worthwhile projects and not be forced to make decisions about money."

Understand? It's important to her, and she tries to get it out before the sun goes down. "If you have the opportunity . . . you know? I mean, to do meaningful work . . . well, that's the thing to do. And that's the thing that scares me . . . if I have to stand up . . . make decisions about the right thing to do at the right moment . . . to maintain stardom . . . or what's good for me . . . wow! When you get successful you have to pay so much more attention, and think things out a lot more clearly . . . just because you want to work. I'm just a bit frightened by all that's happened to me since *Annie Hall* opened. . . ."

By now, you understand that darling Diane clutters her conversation in a confusion of interrupted thoughts that make perfect sense when you're looking into her downy-soft eyes, but leave me puzzled when trying to punctuate her babble. Beneath the wafting tones of disorganized speech, I sense a genuine fear of the naked exposure that accompanies stardom. "I've never been hampered by a high public profile," she continues. "I could walk down any street and do anything and maybe somebody would say 'Hey, you were OK in *The Godfather*,' and that was fine. But to be roughed up and pushed around by fans would be a nightmare. What has that got to do with real life? It's crazy. I don't think that will ever happen to me, because I'm not, after all"— sneaking a giggle—"Farrah Fawcett-Majors. I don't think I'll ever have her public image. I'm an actress, not a fad. I don't think I stand out in a crowd. I don't have a prominent face, or all that hair or all those teeth. I mean, I've got hair and teeth, but—" Keaton's giggle has turned into a full-bodied, vitamin-soaked laugh and at that minute, I'm thinking I could zanily spend the rest of my life with her never finishing a sentence.

"My good friend Carol Kane—she stands out. Her face is . . . uh . . . unique. When we go out together people go crazy over her, and never notice me. Thank goodness. I would hate it, because you never again see the world in its proper perspective. When you make a movie in Hollywood—not Woody's movies, 'cause he's another trip—you get treated like a star with limousines, hairdressers, makeup men . . . all that has nothing to do with real life, either. You get used to the fuss and then when you have to go back to real life, it's hard. In movies, they only worry about whether you're happy, because they think that's the only way you can act. On the stage, they worry about whether you're prepared and if you've got any talent. Movies are weird."

She used to have to audition for roles. Then she met Woody Allen and things got easier. Every actress in Hollywood read for *Looking for Mr. Goodbar*, but Richard Brooks saw something vulnerable in her comedy films and grabbed her, to everyone's amazement, without an audition. "The script is wonderful, but tough. It's a very masochistic part. I had a hard time doing it because I kept wanting the character to change and not go back into another singles bar to pick up another man. This woman is an emotional cripple, incapable of having a relationship with anyone. I think it's going to be a strong, powerful film, and I learned so much from Richard Brooks. He's crazy as a loon—but very affectionate, hilarious, dear and wonderful. No, Woody never came near the set. Richard Brooks closes his sets and he means everybody keep out, including Woody."

She says after the emotionally draining experience of *Looking for Mr. Goodbar* she was "glad to get home to my own dishes again. Boy, I hope life never gets so complicated that I don't do my own dishes. Having maids and help around makes me very uncomfortable. I always have to get up early when the maid comes. So I'd rather be alone, and get up early, do everything fast, then get back into bed for the day, guiltless. Isn't that silly? I live with two cats, lots of plants and my darkroom. I love photography and working with my hands. Photography is better than acting because I can do it alone. I have a great feeling for the visual arts. I don't have the talent to be a painter, but I make great collages. All I need is a glue pot."

A sudden idea hits her. "I should sign up for a course in something visual . . . I enrolled in a print-making course last summer in Greenwich Village, but when I got there I was so threatened by it I couldn't go into the classroom . . . all of my psychological problems got in the way. . . . Too bad . . . I would like to know how that stuff is done . . . maybe one day." She's being wistful.

No one is more charming and vulnerable when wistful than this spacy wisp of a WASP who has been co-star, friend and constant companion to Woody Allen until recently. *Annie Hall* is clearly an autobiographical outcome of their intimate relationship—and its unhappy-happy-unresolved ending.

Whatever you call life's liaisons—affairs, marriages, relationships—when they end, they are simply, sadly over. But Keaton and Allen have had a rare opportunity to live theirs once, go back, rewrite it, film it and live it again—on the screen. I'm reminded of a dear friend who, heartbroken at the end of a long love affair, cried, "What will I do with seven years of home movies?" "Why," answered her shrink, "don't you run them through again and see where you made your mistakes?"

I wondered aloud if *Annie Hall* wasn't a bit like taking that advice. Was making it ever emotionally embarrassing for her and Woody? Diane's answer was short and immediate. *"Yes!"* Then silence. Her decision (Do I go on with this line of thought?) was forming. I could almost hear the thoughts, like tiny ice crystals, tinkling in her mind. "It is always embarrassing to reveal my personal life . . . but emotional embarrassment is a condition of acting . . . revealing yourself even when you're not playing your own life . . . the biggest worry I had making *Annie Hall* was whether or not I would get in my own way. I was afraid that unconsciously I might stop myself from showing the truth because it made me uncomfortable. But"—she shrugs—"the whole process of acting is uncomfortable anyway."

She worries too much about what "they" will say—audiences, critics, unknown phantoms. "All of this is a great time-waster that gets in the way of a performance. I wanted to do *Annie Hall* fully, without worrying what I did wrong in real life. Understand? I had to stop fantasizing about what kind of person I am. Am I bad? Was I wrong in that situation? Did I hurt Woody too much? Was I selfish? There were so many conflicts. But in the final analysis, working out my relationship with Woody was, and still is, great fun, and always a surprise and a revelation to me."

Is it over? "Look . . . Woody and I . . . we're beyond getting involved again with each other . . . and beyond really hurting each other, which is a wonderful place to get with someone you love . . . there's humor, affection and a certain dependency between us. He's my closest and dearest friend. The only other situation I know like ours—where a movie was made of the actors' off-screen affair—was *Made for Each Other* with Renée Taylor and Joe Bologna. That was a comedy, too, but with sharp edges."

She obviously has a neurotic love-hate relationship with acting, but says forlornly, "I don't know what I'd do without it. I'd be in a pickle." She's kinky but proper, a well-bred all-American girl hiding behind funky shades, just like Annie Hall. "My real name is Hall, but when I registered with Actors' Equity they made me change it because there already was a Diane Hall. I took my mother's maiden name, Keaton. In the beginning—and this is interesting, psychologically—I took my sister's name, Dorrie. After six months it dawned on me how terrible I was . . . after all, Dorrie was *her* name . . . she *is* Dorrie Hall . . . I think I did it because I like her and thought her good qualities would rub off on me, but if I was a flop as an actress, all the bad reviews would be going to *her*. . . ."

Keaton also has a granny, just like the one in the film, "with the greatest sense of humor . . . I love her so . . . I was raised in Santa Ana . . . John Birch country . . . California . . . I'm still smitten with the horizontal view . . . I have such wonderful memories of my childhood in the desert. . . . Woody hates California and is unrelenting about how much he despises it, but to me Hollywood is not California. I couldn't take Hollywood any more than Woody could . . . Joan Didion also hates California . . . God, how I wish I could work with her someday . . . remember *Play It As It Lays* with Tuesday Weld? Isn't Tuesday great? She plays my sister in *Looking for Mr. Goodbar* and she's great . . . I love Tuesday. . . ."

When the defenses are down and the chasm widens, she talks a blue streak. "Do you think I look like Loretta Young? But she was so beautiful . . . oh, I wish I could see all of her movies, not just the ones on TV . . . hey, listen, maybe you can tell me why . . . Irene Dunne . . . oh, wow! . . . She's someone I love . . . what a wonderful comedienne . . . such style, wit and bite. Funny, isn't it, those who remain stars always, and those who fade into memory . . . well, I gotta go now."

The cowboy hat is once more produced and she slowly tucks the straggling hair under its crown. "Nothing is happening next . . . I have no films lined up. . . . Maybe I'll get to take that visual arts class . . . that would be nice. . . ." A tiny wave of the hand sends Keaton off into the rain. Nobody notices as she passes through the crowded luncheonette. Only the waitress comments, "That crazy kid gonna get drenched without an umbrella."